CW01594505

POETRY
now

BARDS AROUND BRITAIN

Edited by

Liz Wakefield

First published in Great Britain in 1997 by
POETRY NOW
1-2 Wainman Road, Woodston,
Peterborough, PE2 7BU
Telephone (01733) 230746
Fax (01733) 230751

HB ISBN 1 86188 773 6
SB ISBN 1 86188 778 7

FOREWORD

Although we are a nation of poetry writers we are accused of not reading poetry and not buying poetry books: after many years of listening to the incessant gripes of poetry publishers, I can only assume that the books they publish, in general, are books that most people do not want to read.

Poetry should not be obscure, introverted, and as cryptic as a crossword puzzle: it is the poet's duty to reach out and embrace the world.

The world owes the poet nothing and we should not be expected to dig and delve into a rambling discourse searching for some inner meaning.

The reason we write poetry (and almost all of us do) is because we want to communicate: an ideal; an idea; or a specific feeling. Poetry is as essential in communication, as a letter; a radio; a telephone, and the main criteria for selecting the poems in this anthology is very simple: they communicate.

This collection of poetry is written by everyday people from all over Britain. They have come together to represent the standard of poetry which is being written today.

The poems inside are extremely varied, some complex, some simple but all of them communicate directly with the reader. The poems cover a wide variety of subjects from the traditional such as love and peace to the more modern issues of the environment and politics. All of the poems are written from the heart and some show thoughts and emotions which are often hard to express in any other way.

This is a diverse collection of poetry which will be enjoyed by all who read it.

Contents

A School Pet

A rabbit, no a goldfish, no a bear
A bear would be a great idea give all the teachers a scare
Maybe a lion a tiger too, soon were going to be able
To open a zoo
A monkey or two might do the trick
A scorpion too, that should give a nasty sharp prick
A few tarantulas will just do brill
Maybe there'll give the teachers a thrill
Spiders, woodlice, flies and worms
Maybe we'll get an early half-term
I hope you all know we all like this stuff
It should make the teachers vanish in a puff.

Lucy Firth

Forget Me Not

Christmas is a festive time, people rally round,
Presents adorn the trees, which we put them round
Homes decked out with nativity scenes,
Children pray that Santa answers their dreams.
Some people cast a festive cheer,
Others sing carols for people to hear.
Let's not forget the twenty-fifth of December,
Peace and kindness we remember.
Spare a thought, the festive times in mind,
The reason for celebrating, in the bible you will always find.

John P Evans

John Lennon Was My Idol

John Lennon was my friend
John Lennon the musician
Wrote many songs and sang
He used to live in Liverpool
The Cavern was his den.
John Lennon was my idol
John Lennon was my friend
He moved away from Liverpool
The Cavern and his den
Across the sea to America
To write more verse and song
New York he stayed with Yoko
John Lennon the musician
And there he fell prey of an assassin
John Lennon the musician
John Lennon was my idol
John Lennon was my friend
John Lennon is no more.

Trevor Watmuff

Celestial (Moon And Star)

As sisterly companions
They keep their vigil
A symbol of nature
That emits a vivid
Light of splendour
Whose night peace
Allures the sweetest
Birdcall

Irene Gunnion

SAM

'Hello', I'm a dog
And my name is Sam,
I'm all alone
For I haven't a mam.

The people I lived with
Have all gone away,
And I'm here in this home
Just another stray.

They bought me for Christmas
I didn't cost much,
There were kisses and cuddles
They made such a fuss.

They've moved now
And they've thrown me out,
But before they went
They gave me a clout.

It's not too bad here
They do their best,
But I'm just a stray
Like all the rest.

But some day, someone may come
And say 'Oh look he's just what we wanted,'
Then I can sleep
And feel once more contented.

William A Stowe

AWAKENING

Crisp leaves carpet the red walk, crunching towards the dog
Free bridges crossing the stream of clear water washing a
thousand years of patterns onto the veined stones, some lightly
covered with lichen, painting a message understood by the few.
Small adventurous shoots glimpse the world conned by a warm
Air flow, or reading the weather accurately, a promise of spring.
Listen for the call of the marauding cuckoo; watching for the
Return of the dancing swallow, who dive-bombs midges; the pied
Wagtail pauses on a washed stone and proudly displays to his
Mate, a world apart, his world of the woods, free of torment, but
Hide from the sparrow hawk! Free of ambition, a clean clear
Life of procreation . . .
The bluebell beds spread everywhere, prolific, robust waiting
The time to boast their glory in constant blue.
The waterfall isn't smashing into he stream just yet, but
Throwing glancing blows awaiting the rains of early spring,
When there will be a place for the dipper to hunt and the robins
To build safely behind in the clefts of rock hidden from
Searching eyes.
Scuttling rabbits tell of the fox silently watching from the hill.
Wondering whether he'll make the dash before they reach
The safety of their burrows. His piercing eyes, lightly twitching
Nose he knows he can't win today . . . but the woods are his living
Room and he knows every mark like a nana in a kitchen . . He'll wait.
The sun picks its rays through the thickening trees, a tube
Of glistening light warms the earth . . . the woodland awakes, the
Orchestra of songbirds entertain: a new season begins in coed
Bach.

Robert King

SATURDAY NIGHT AND SUNDAY MORNING

The young girl curls in her feminine bed
She had danced into the early hours
Mesmerised by the hot hall
And the flashing excitement of lights
And then
With the final discordant sound
It was home
With her jangled memories of the night slowly fading
Fading like the last kisses that had bruised her lips

The young girl curls in her feminine bed
And sighs in her dreams as young men rise
Dancing and smiling
Saturday night fevering
Everyone as handsome as sin

Here comes the sun
The early sparrows din over a morning crumb
The girl sleeps on

She wakes now and yawns into Sunday
Her mother enters
With unspoken questions and a hidden fear
The girl remembers her Saturday night
She stretches
Smiles
Her mother nods and suddenly remembers
Her mother with her hidden fear

The girl rises
And goes down
To a frowning father

John Jones

GRANDAD

'Tell me again, Grandad.
Tell me again.'
Then we'd fall about laughing
and all about nothing.
Then Nanna would say,
'You're just being silly.'
Then we'd roll about laughing
and it was all about nothing.
Then there was a day
when he just looked tired,
as pale as the sheets in the
outside lane.
I played by our rules.
Hiding in doorways.
He knew I was there but he just
walked on by and sat himself,
down in the chair.
He didn't laugh in that loud
jovial manner but a soft smile
and a finger pointing, told me
I was spotted.
Then he just stared back across the room,
as though he was waiting.
So that's what I told me Nan and me Mum.
Out in the backyard, I kicked at the chalk stone
I'd previously used to write on the wall.
Looked in through the window, looking for Grandad.
What could be wrong, wasn't he well?
I tapped at the window to show off my drawings,
to show off the mess I'd just made in the yard.
One look at Mum's face as she drew the curtains,
spiralled me back and out the back gate.
And I sat on the ground with my hand on my head,
searching for the words that Grandad last said.
But there was nothing, but a heart full of pain.

Later, with Mum, on the hospital green,
I vigorously waved to the window Mum pointed.
A smile tried to push aside a soft stream of tears
and the lingering memory of Grandad and me.
The early years.

Antony Gilbert

So Cold The Night

The frost that glistens all around,
The spiders' webs, so well made, glow.
Their little hearts beat so fast.

The fox runs wild, above,
To escape the hunters claws,
For them, survival is the only law,
They have no points to score.
They fight only their own war.

Watching them all here,
Far away from strangers' eyes,
So near though, to their lies.
I wonder what I should say,
I don't like the games the govenment play.

To fight for queen and country is okay for some,
Guess I'm learning my lesson there.
I need someone to care,
It would be nice for someone to be there,
I ain't no loner,
And all I want is my fair share.

John Hughes

Strawberry Time

June has arrived, warm days and light evenings. I love this time of year. Driving through the country roads, we see the bright red poppies with their delicate heads dancing with the wild daisies along the side of the road. The aroma of strawberries from the local farm, tell us they are ready to be picked in abundance, by car loads of families. Then, bowed down with their various vessels, filled and overflowing, they have them weighed.

Like a flock of birds heading home, all of a sudden the peace comes back to the countryside and the ticking of time winds itself down to a warm dusty evening.

Yvette Kuipers

A Dog

A dog is like a log
When it has a sleep,
A dog is like a child
When it's at your feet.

A dog is most obedient.
It'll come to you when you call,
A dog is most courageous
It'll help you if you fall.

A dog is very smelly
When it does get wet,
A dog is mans best friend
So it's perfect for a pet.

Russell Charles Franklin

THE CHRISTMAS PARTY

Tonight's our Christmas party, so welcome one and all
For without our friends and family it wouldn't be Christmas at all
It's a time for giving and sharing, a time to show that we care
With all the warmth and goodwill for everyone to share.
There's a wonderful smell of baking, there's a tree with its baubles
and lights
And the beautiful sound of carols that rends the cold frosty night.
Yet we ladies we sigh and we grumble, there's such a lot to do
With cards to write and presents to wrap, we think that we'll never
get through.
But somehow or other we manage and exclaim - never again!
Yet we know when it comes around next year
We'll do it all over again.

Barbara E Rowley-Blake

SCHOOL REPORT

Philip's
a
tryer
and is reading well - the best reader
in class, in fact. However, his
written work is poor as
he's lacking in
grammar.
Nor is
he good with maths.
It's as though he's living in a
dreamworld - he often seems
preoccupied. Though he has taken a
very keen interest this year in his form teacher,
Miss Goodbody's Art and Design!

Philip Johnson

Grandma And Her Garden

For her, the garden is the place
Where life in miniature is found.
The trials and joys of life itself
are rooted there. And in the ground
she strives to make a happy home
for all her children plants.

The woman's work is never done -
each season brings new toil,
a constant battle must be won
to clear the weeds and free the soil,
so that her youngsters have a chance
to put down roots and grow-up
tall and beautiful.

No garden apron, gloves or trendy gear
are needed by this Mother Eve
Down on her knees she does not fear
to plunge bare hands into the earth and leave
it cleaner by her touch

For her, 'adopted children' plants
deserve especial care.
Some come from friends or aged aunts
and some are 'picked' from who knows where.
But all are quickly bedded in
and made to feel at home.

And year by year as they grow up,
She notes their changing features
Some need a trim, some must be moved
and washed to rid them of those minute creatures
which hide beneath the leaves.

Her favourite saying is to quote,
while brandishing a spade,
a couplet from a poet who wrote
'For gardens are not made
by saying *oh how beautiful*
and sitting in the shade!'

Ken Whitelock

THE VIS-IT

From whence it came, nobody knew,
It just appeared 'Out of the Blue'
Some said it 'Were devil, in disguise,'
Others said it 'Had been planted by Russian spies.'

Women and children stayed in at night,
And many a man admitted to fright.
Curtains were drawn throughout the town,
And all public places had to close down.

An emergency meeting of town council was called,
And the Lady Mayoress said that she was appalled,
That it had come without warning, nothing at all,
No letter, no fax, no telephone call.

All councillors present, at long last agreed,
That whatever was done it must be with speed,
But members were tired and the hour was late,
So an adjournment was called for some other date.

Lights went out early, the townspeople slept,
In darkness they heard it and out of bed leapt.
Curtains were opened and lights were put on,
And as they peered through their windows,
They saw 'It' had gone!

Brian Greaves

HARD SELL

The caller, he was quite amazed
We didn't wish to be double-glazed,
He wrote our names down in his book,
Gave us a searching second look.

Persistently he tried again
Standing there in driving rain,
'Let me come and demonstrate,
I'm open to negotiate.

Three windows for the price of two,
A further discount just for you,
Your heating bills will soar no more,'
His foot moved closer to the door.

We shook our heads, we weren't inclined,
But he determined in his mind
To try once more to make a sale,
Hoping that he would not fail.

'Ten minutes, not a moment more,
You'll be persuaded I am sure,
These windows I can guarantee
Are quite superior quality.'

We sighed and looked him in the eye,
He really tried to make us buy,
We said, 'Sorry, this is not your day,
We're selling up to move away.'

Carol Mansfield

Silent Music

The horse and plough carved the earth, Man sowed the seed.
As I walked up a narrow quiet lane, near where I live, enjoying
warm sunshine and light breeze.
I was aware of the sun glistening on the dark green corn, and obeying
natures movement of warming breeze and leaning, bending, swaying
to and fro. Continually.
I looked across the field and not to its length.
Nature the source, the living world. Had raised her unseen wand the
wind, and a million green ears.
Responded giving a rhapsody of silent music blending and yet
contrasting to a nearby hill hedge, white blue sky and flitting birds.
I drank this in. This silent green moving music.
Finally, I walked away.
Privileged and in awe of her wholeness and her sharing for us all.

John Wentworth

Crossmaglen 1973

Green rain rolls like gunfire
Across the hills and fires the streets,
And in its spate
We learn to hate the market squares
Where once cattle stood.
Now hawk squadrons settle
And staring houses that metal
With tongues of fire,
Spit upon the cassocks of our calling
Where we tread the pain filled
Hassocks of another world.

Martin Clark

THE DANCE

The music from the bagpipes skirl as round the hall the
dancers whirl,
Round and round and in and out, with mighty leaps and
hearty shouts;
The colours of the Tartans blend, as lines of dancers
twist and bend.
It seems as though their feet have wings as ever faster
now they spin.
At last the dances end draws near and soon the dancers
with a cheer
Salute their partners, walk away, until once more at end
of day
The lonely Piper's sad lament, wafts out across tall
tenements
To bid goodnight, farewell to all, then slowly into
silence fall,
And only mist will fill the glen, until the dancers
come again.

Winifred Jenkins

FRIENDS ARE THERE WHEN YOU NEED THEM!

Why weren't you there when I needed help?
Why didn't you come and see me?
Why didn't you ring?
Why did you only write once?

You were my oldest friend,
But I don't consider you my friend anymore,
For friends are there when you need them and you were not there!

H R Laden

The Sea Of Life

The sea of life has tossed me onto some strange and foreign shore
The winds whipped all around me and left me lost and sore
I'm stranded on an island, don't know which way to go
There is no boat to take me I'm feeling very low
There is no signpost for a road to lead me on my way
No guide to take me by the hand, give comfort day by day
I must find the map that charts the way ahead
To get me where I'm comfortable and not in fear and dread
There must be a guiding star in the heavens above
To lead me to a harbour of happiness and love
Where the sea of life is calm and gentle breezes blow
And I can drop my anchor and once more start to grow.

Sheila Haggerty

Winter Trees

Upon a downland hilltop high
The trees stand stark and bare,
Outlined against a sunset sky,
Its colours rich and rare.
No longer clothed in summer green,
Nor yet in autumn gold,
But black with resting starlings
Looking bleak and somehow old.
Then later, dressed in winter snow,
Frost diamonds in their hair,
They stand in all their beauty
Like princesses tall and fair.

Dede Banks

A Birthday Wish

This morning you are just eighteen.
Some ways this makes me sad.
No longer will you be all mine
I know, and yet I'm glad
That you will face life with a smile
Secure in faith and love -
With friends and folks around you
Who trust you - and who'll prove
That this is what life's all about
To fulfil every minute,
To give, to try, to trust in God
And live it - to the limit.

Catherine R Thomas

Nations Not Apart

I came from Erin's shores
To England's heartland dark
I left the Irish bigotry,
Unfairness, class ridden
Society less a purpose.
Erin's lovely landscape
Not to be matched afar,
Across the water rough
Pagan England, you serve
Us proud as we deserve.
Our blame we can throw
But we always know
Thank God there's an England

Merrick Power

MEMORIES

Everything changes, nothing stays the same
Why do we always think the good times will remain?

The times we exchanged recipes, those happy get-togethers.
Visiting each other every week, in all sorts of weather.

Those days sewing and knitting, or planting little seeds
Nurturing and watering to meet our gardens needs.

And now your garden's glorious, but you're not there to tend
'All things bright and beautiful,' we miss you
Our Dearest Friend

Dorothy Noonan

PRECIOUS BUBBLE

Life is like a bubble floating
on the air
It can sail along without worry
or care
If you try to chase it as it floats
in space
You can catch up with it and it
pops in your face.

It can have beautiful pictures of
pink and blue
It depends how you form it and
exude it from you,
So cup it gently and savour
whilst you can
For we are only a bubble in life's
plan.

Sylvia Olliver

STONE WALLS

Stone walls provide a habitat
Beneath stone crop that forms a mat
Insects and lizards hide below
Where scabious and foxglove grow

Whinberries grow at the base
Ivy twines along the face
From crevices, hang purple heather
Where sheep shelter from the weather

A thriving miniature community
That we humans rarely see
Man built, so the sheep can't roam
Stone walls, wildlife makes a home

Bridget Eyre

MY UNCLE COL

This is an ode to my uncle Col
There are many things that make him special
But I can't name them all
The list would be as long
As the bike ride to the shops
Can you remember that?
The list would be as endless
As the amount of times you have seen Sheffield United play
Have you ever seen them win?
My uncle Col is so special to me
He is the best uncle I have got
You are my one and only uncle Col
And the best one anyone could ever wish for.

Sarah Jones-Davies (12)

Dogged Chum

He introduced himself with a wag of his tail
Scampered around us with a low soft growl
We smiled, patted his head, but please take note
Not all of us felt inclined to stroke or dote
on your mischievous yapping ball of fluff
When he rifled our biscuit tin he called our bluff

We shook our heads, muttered 'He's not house trained'
Why did you scowl at us, you looked so pained.
With puddles on our carpet we'd really had enough
of your naughty puppy dog, it was time to be tough

We called a general meeting, discussed what to do
Now we all like him better, when he obeys you
Still a rogue, your best friend an artful dodger
But we all agree he's now the best kind of lodger

A true friend to all of those that he knows
But beware if you are one of his foes.

Sheila Pharo

Pippa

Pippa lazed in the warm summer sun.
Today was a rest day - a day made for fun.
Later perhaps she'd go for a stroll;
Rest awhile on a grassy knoll.
Back home again in time for tea;
Spend the evening on the new settee.
Tomorrow she'll be back on duty -
Work for her brains and not her beauty.
But she never found this to be a bind,
Working as a Guide Dog for the Blind.

Gerald Law

CHOICES

Friday New signpost in the village,
Kitschy. Toytown-twee.
With cutesy Olde World lettering,
White on azure. Three
Slender arms that point the way
To river, downs or sea.

A snow-bound, silent midnight.
I've got the big-time blues.
Snug in Shetland sweater,
Cords and sturdy shoes
I stand before the signpost.
Which walk should I choose?

Sunday Floating through the empty streets
In the wake of dawn,
I feel so light, so loose of limb,
Ethereal, new-born.
Then, passing the newsagents,
Among the Sunday porn.

A front-page story strikes my eyes;
'Shock Discovery'
Body found on riverbank!
And, oh, *how could it be?*
Beneath the screaming headline
Is a photograph
of
Me . . .

Elizabeth Mark

BULLYING

Oh! Sir, it was only a joke,
I only gave that fat lad a poke.
You girl why do you stare,
All I did was pull your hair.
Let's get him he's on his break,
See how much punching he'll take.
Squeeze his arm make him yell,
It's okay he won't tell.
Oh! Look at him his face looks funny,
Come on let's see if he's got any money.
I do have teachers who really care.
But try and tell them if you dare.
I know I'll get it the following day,
In the toilets or playground they'll make me pay.
Why are people so cruel and unkind,
I know it's not something in my mind.
I may be different in shape or size,
Or frizzy hair and different eyes.
But we have feelings that still count,
So *think!* Next time before you *hit out!*

Linda Woodhouse

HEALTHY

If you want to be healthy,
Eat lots of fruit and veg,
Do your exercises daily,
And get lots of sleep in bed,
Being healthy can be good,
Although some veg doesn't taste nice,
But eat lots of this type of food,
And you'll be alive and healthy.

Heather Stansfield (11)

HEDGEHOG

A small, brown, spiky ball lies in the middle of a road,
It bursts all the tyres that carry a heavy load,
Eventually, someone stops to think
And takes it home to have a drink,
They take it to the vet
And ask to keep it as a pet,
But, they have been told
To let it out in the wild,
And not to treat it as a child,
So, if you want to show a hedgehog love,
You will do everything above.

Julie-Anne McCann (10)

TWOPENNY CHIC

Dress up to kill
dress up to the nines
the nifty nineties
are waiting for you.

Ties are old hat,
suits are worn with boots.

Obey the 'Dress Code' means:
No trainers, no jeans!
Or, know the bouncer.

Oxfam's okay for clothes
but a bit expensive for the
Twopenny Chic.

Danny Wise

POEMS

Maybe I'll write one tomorrow,
Perhaps then the urge will creep over me,
Maybe I'll write one tomorrow,
Anyhow I'll just wait and see,
My mind is blank of ideas now,
I must let my thoughts all run free,
My mind is blank of ideas now,
But the problem won't let me be.

To put pen to paper to rhyme well,
For a deadline at the end of July,
To put pen to paper to rhyme well,
I'll give it a really good try,
The charity's such a good cause mind,
But gosh how time it does fly,
The charity's such a good cause mind,
But my thoughts all keep passing me by.

It's no good! - But hey look! I've done it,
Hooray for Guide dogs for the blind.

June Prescott

SHOO! SCARY SPIDER

Susie's scared stupid,
She shakes and shivers,
Screams and shrieks,
She spots spider,
Scuttling and scurrying,
Scarper, scary spider,
Shouldn't stay,
So shift soon,
So Susie sleeps sound.

Alison Mary Petrie

ODE TO A SUPER QUARRY

These are my mountains
And this is my glen,
All to be blown up
By greedy men
Who want a motorway
From Bologne to Hong Kong.
Ballast from their bulk carriers
Gives our sea quite a pong!
It poisons our shellfish
And puts the salmon all wrong.

Oh these were my mountains
And this was my glen -
They've all gone away,
Thanks to these greedy men.
Jobs for the boys?
Perhaps a few for the locals
Whose lungs are now dust-filled
And they've lost all their vocals.
What are we left with?
Just a dirty big hole
Full of the gas radon
Which of our lungs, takes its toll.

Oh where are the tourists?
There are no views to view.
It looks like the planners
Have just left us to stew.
Oh where are my mountains?
Somewhere in Europe, perhaps Japan
Maybe in Asia or even Siam.
I wish I had protested
Oh wa ta foo liam!

Alan E Joyce

ELUSIVE BUTTERFLY

A delightful sight catches my eye
As dainty wings go fluttering by
I've never seen a beauty fly
As graceful as a butterfly.

I watch in fear as small hands try
To catch one as it's drifting by,
And jump with joy each time they miss
That butterfly, I'd love to kiss.

Across the fields and sloping hills
There's miles of golden daffodils
I stroll along with eager eye
I'm searching for a butterfly.

My feathered friends content on wing
Pleasure my heart each time they sing
With upturned head I breathe a sigh
Where are you elusive butterfly?

Phyllis R Harvey

FIRST DAY

There, there, don't be upset, dry your tears,
You mustn't let the others see you crying.
School is really an exciting place.
Look, we have a Wendy House and Nature Table,
We're going to play with sand and water,
And finger painting is great fun,
We'll learn to read and deal with numbers.
You won't be parted very long,
Dinner-time will come before you know it.
Feeling better? I'm so glad,
See you at twelve, then, Mrs Strong!

B Gordon

I SHOULD HAVE EATEN SOMETHING

I'm famished
I'm starving
I'm losing weight
I'm ill
I'm feeling weak
I'm feeling tired
I'll take another pill
I should have eaten something
It's not too late right now
I'm going to have a damn good lunch
A pick-me-up, and how
And now I've over-eaten
I'm feeling quite ill
I might be feeling stronger
But I'll take another pill
I need a dietician
To tell me how to eat
I need a dietician
To tell me when to eat
And no longer undernourished
A dietician I must meet
A sign of health
Then I would be
When walking down the street
So proud, so proud
And happy now
I've never felt so good
I've been advised
And done exactly what I should.

Melvyn Roiter

Thwarted Ambition

I wish that I could write real poetry
Like Shakespeare, Wordsworth, Shelley, Keats or Burns
Expressing deep emotions in blank verse
Or sonnets with their complicated form.

At second best I could aspire
To be a comic versifier
Aping the Gilbertian wit;
Or having a recording hit
With songs accompanied on
A piano played by Donald Swann.

I could string my words together
In 'odd odes' like Cyril Fletcher
Or make lines of rhyming pairs
In the manner of Pam Ayres.

Perhaps I could make rhymes outlandish,
And have it said I'm Ogden Nash-ish.

But, alas, I know it's not in me to be a poet.
I can only create doggerel -
Which doesn't scan, or even make a decent rhyme with
William McGonagal.

Mike Smith

Friends

Friends are partners in the rough,
Friends are apples on the trees,
Friends feel each other's pain,
Friends are with each other,
What I and many others like about
Friends, is just the way they are.

Luke Spencer (12)

THE NEW FOREST

Fir trees seen in sunlight's warmth
Dark, silent sentinels by moonlight's chill.
In the hollows, 'neath the groves
Bats and pixies dwell.
Neon-lit mirroring of the stars, show off
Glowworms light the dark.

Feared he is of hunting men
Hunger driven fox deserts his den,
Wild ponies cropping in the night
Neigh and sniff the pinewood air
Whilst dapple deer shiver shy
When ghostly knights ride softly by.

The tale is told of Rufus Stone
Of men, hounds and killing.
The Battle of Hastings William won
But here in the forest lost his first son.
From Tyrrell's bow an arrow sped
Killing King William in his chest.

Beaulieu Abbey once stood strong
Built it was by good King John.
Now abandoned by monks who fled
The Latin Mass no longer said.
Sad forlorn they rest their heads
Beneath the burial stones.

F B Rylance

My Time Machine

Where does the time go? It simply seems to fly.
I never seem to have enough, and no matter how I try,
I always have a 'back log' - not of domestic chores
that I manage all right, I've not got unswept floors.
All my corners are clean and dusting has been done
but I have to be determined to leave time for a bit of fun.
Not wild parties I'm planning - just time for the things I enjoy
like pottery, writing poetry, reading, gardening - I can't afford
to employ
some one to do those mundane jobs like sweeping the path or
cutting grass
or changing a fuse or a light bulb. I'm a versatile old lass
but, now, my hands are stiffening and every task takes me longer
and the frightening thing is that I know I won't get any stronger
Though, as long as I am healthy and do not break a bone
and am able to do my job of work and afford to talk on the phone
I will be delighted. I'm just slower to get started
It is true that an active old age is reserved for the stout hearted.
It takes me until February to catch up that we're in another year
and the weeks speed past like a jet plane or a racing car in eighth gear.
I thought there'd be time to contemplate and spend time
counting blessings
but the dates change so fast on the calendar they just leave me guessing.
I try to keep an engagement diary not because I live in a social whirl
but I'm so forgetful these days - the scroll seems to unfurl
at such a pace I can't keep up and I don't want to fall behind,
I've never been ambitious to lead a race but nowadays I find
increasingly the tempo of life is getting right out of hand,
I won't give in till I have to and I hope you'll understand
that I'm not really complaining - I just find it slightly bewildering
and my time machine needs repairing or even, perhaps, rebuilding.

F B O'Brien

Memories Of Pepi

Pepi you really looked a sight
Your fur was matted you looked a fright
I know you didn't have a very good start
That is how you captured my heart
I couldn't tell your head from your tail
You were so thin and very frail
You were so nervous you used to jump
When anything was dropped or you heard a thump
Just give him time the vet used to say
And in the end you started to play
A little black poodle showing off
Collecting the toys I used to toss
You gave eleven years of joys and sorrows
Now you're gone no more tomorrows
Pepi I won't forget those days
Photographs and memories on every page
Of an album dedicated to you
For the love you gave me
Though the years were few.

J R Bayliss

Perception

I am a skyscraper
When my hair falls out it spirals to the floor
As discarded paper from a forty-third floor
My eyes in their sockets
Are like spacemen in rockets
Staring down at my earth-bound feet
If my head fell off they'd have a different angle
Looking up like a man on the street.

Graham Robert Mann

The Rainforest

Humming birds and epiphytes,
Free-tailed bats that fly at nights.
Hornbills, indris, pangolins,
Golden pottos, manakins,
Dusky langurs, civet cats,
Rattlesnakes and tube-nosed bats.
Chrysomelids, carpenter bees,
God made the rainforests for these.
Pig-tailed macaques, viverrids,
Woolly monkeys, tabanids,
Heliconid butterflies, collugos,
Jacamars and curasows.
Indians with handmade tools
Who live according to the rules,
But, selfish we do far exceed
And take beyond the things we need:
Deprive the earth of Nature's store;
Requiring more, and ever more.
Despoiling, killing what is good
To satisfy our thirst for wood.
Humming birds and epiphytes,
A million other wondrous sights,
Eliminating, one by one,
Until at last they'll all be gone.
What will remain? Want to guess?
Civilised man and one big mess:
Climatic change; greenhouse effect;
Catastrophes that can't be checked;
Deserts spreading far and wide -
A recipe for homicide.

Eric Roy Chapman

Cricket 1997

Summer times are creeping in again
With beating, burning sun and rain
And so with all these longer brighter days
Cricket comes to bring its joyous ways.
Now for this aged, doddering coach,
Sunday morning and Monday eve approach;
Week upon week the kids' demands be set,
Filling three hours or so whene'er they met
The game's the thing with drinks of cola
And biscuits served, first innings is over.
One more innings to fit in to the time:
And when it's done, who clears the grime
Those kids have left on our pavilion floor?
The fate of the manager, lock the door
Then take those kids back to their places;
Summer is the burden of the graces.

John Hall

Cats

Cats slip like water through
your hands,
they climb up fences jump
in tubs,
They're friendly little tiger cubs!

They're playful silly sleek and slow,
With eyes like pearls all aglow

Ears that point all around,
Their small tails on the ground.

Fluffy balls of feline fur,
Hear those tiny kittens purr!

Emma Beswick (13)

Sizzle Time

Heat cracks the ground,
which then snaps like twigs,
willows of wasps invade the air.
They congregate around sticky
wrappers and dustbin lids,
as they relate to playground bullies.
Children's clothes peel off like
banana skins,
revealing white pulpy skin.
All common-sense is corroded by
the sun.
We yield to the rays and welcome
sizzle time.
Like a barbecue we slowly turn
in the heat,
displaying all colours under the sun.
Ozone degeneration; but still we
don't stop.
What is not seen cannot end this dream,
our blisters are blissfully unaware,
as we lie in sizzle time,
creating skin disease.

Lorraine Johns

Famous

Wouldn't it be nice if I were famous,
Singing songs, all different types,
Standing on stage with really big crowds,
Hearing lots of people giving off screams and shouts,
Seeing lots of lads with 'I love you' flags,
Feeling mighty nervous, but really really glad,
Knowing all the words but still thinking I'll forget,
Time to go on, I'm a nervous wreck.

C L Robertshaw

A Roam Round Town

I roam round town with little cash
And wonder where to go.
Pop in the shops out of the crush
Take shelter from the showers.
Magic word 'Sale' oh boy!
Rush over to the racks with joy.
No cash, but credit card in hand
I wander through the wonderland.

Satin blouses beckon me -
Blue, black, pink and yellow,
T-shirts smile in every style
And every clashing colour.
Let me be out before I fall
There's rent to pay, there's food to find,
Have I the busfare home?
Oh wicked card, I nearly fell
But no-one knows and I won't tell.
Next time I'll leave the card at home
When I get the urge to roam.

Ruth Turner

My Lovely Mum

The world is so big, and I feel so small
I look up at the trees which are very tall
But most of all I'm blessed with a mum
Who will always listen, until kingdom come
She reads stories at night before I sleep
So that my dreams will always be sweet
I can always tell her my sorrows and joys
Which is much better than playing with toys
She often says let me hear you sing
It makes me happy to have her blessing

Patience Millard

TWO FOALS

Foals in a field,
Legs outspread,
'Mid buttercups, daisies
And clover of red.
Looking so beautiful,
Wonderfully made,
Slender and delicate
God's new creation
There displayed.
So trusting and natural
In their mother's love,
May we, like them,
Trust our Father above.
For them life is simple,
Just good being alive,
A feast of adventure,
Learning how to survive.
So be a natural
Child of the King,
Simply trusting His love
In everything.
For Our Father knows
The path that we tread,
So let's give Him our lives,
By Him be led.

PTL

AUTUMN LEAVES

A carpet of crispness, I so cautiously tread.
Colours of yellow, amber and red.
Where do they go to, this abundance of leaves.
That fall very gently, with such graceful ease.

C Sinclair

'Pie' In The Sky

As I lay, I look dreamily into the sky
Fluffy clouds remind me of lemon meringue pie
Others remind me of sweet candyfloss
With a tint of pink right across
Could be strawberry and vanilla, my favourite ice-cream
Or lovely light mousse with a blob of cream
Smaller clouds drift away, none of the big ones
will catch them today
Some like cotton wool thick fluffy and white
Now the clouds have changed to blue, the sun's
shining so bright
The sun disappeared the clouds all gone grey
I think we'll have some rain today
At least that's what forecasters say
Now the clouds are back to brilliant white
The sun behind giving golden rays of light
I love to watch the clouds drift slowly by
Then again I also love the night sky
On a clear summer night stars shining down
Like sparkling sequins on a ball gown.
Search for the Great Bear and Milk Way,
I'm sure I'll see them sometime today
A shooting star whizzes down to Earth
Make a wish for all you're worth
Then a crash of thunder a lightning flash
The rain's on its way sorry must dash
Once inside I watch the forecast storm
Bet it will subside before the dawn
so I can watch the clouds as I lazily yawn.

Sandra Witt

New Shoes

I went to buy a pair of shoes,
They looked nice I did enthuse,
Have you any left in grey,
No, we sold them all yesterday,
Have you any left in brown,
No, try somewhere else in town,
Other shops I tried to no avail,
None at all were on sale,
To the first shop I went back,
Have you any left in black,
Yes sir was the reply,
What size do you wish to try,
I said size ten should be fine,
All they had though was size nine,
Which I bought but never again,
Because I now walk in constant pain.

Martin Westcott

Rain

Damp hedges, silver rain banging on the window
pane like a silver chain.
Puddles to splash in, oh goody.
My anorak is wet, my boots are muddy.
Rain pattering on the ground, a gloomy sky all around.
Rain splashing in the river, I feel cold and start to shiver.
The sky is really dull, now the guttering is very full.
I can't go to the park, when it's wet, but saying
rain's boring is something I regret.
I can splash in the puddles, I can catch rain in my
hand, I don't mind if there's no brass band.

Kelly Cronin (8)

God's Creation

What is it that makes the world go round?
Is it people living in country or in town? Could it be that nature there
with flowers and trees almost everywhere?
Is it the wind blowing north to south or east to west when it's at its best.
Perhaps it's the sun up in the sky with all the clouds flying wide
and high.
The moon and stars in the dark of night, with a meteor occasionally
in full flight.
Perhaps it's a combination of all these things creating movement like
a bird on the wing.
Whatever it is we can thank the Lord up above for the giving of life
with his power and his love.

Clarence Gascoigne

Famous

I want to be famous
Be a name on people's tongue,
I want to be remembered
For something great
That I have done.
Time would mar my gravestone
Be forgotten in the dust,
So to be famous
For me is a must.
I want it known
That I existed,
Made my mark upon the world.
To show my life was vital
And all my dreams unfurled.

Jean Barr

My Dad - The Postman!

Who is this person,
Who rises up at dawn,
And delivers all our letters,
And cards when babes are born.

Who trudges through all kinds of weather,
Come sun, rain or snow,
Or if he really likes it,
We never need to know.

Who always has a cheery smile,
And always says 'Hello!'
Who whistles on his rounds,
He's such a cheery fellow.

Who comes in all shapes and sizes,
He may be just a lad,
Or someone slightly older,
That postman could be my Dad!

Nadine Jacobs

Memories

Looking back on life so far
memories come back like a shining star
Some are happy some are sad
Some I wish I never had
I think of all the folk I've known
And the wild oats I've sown
I met an old friend today
so another memory to put away.

Pamela Butler

Pet Shop Blues

The doctor told the man
To say how he was feeling,
And when the chap began,
His words were most revealing:

'My pet shop is my life,
From early youth I planned it -
How can I face my wife
And say I cannot stand it!

I cannot stand the dogs,
The bunnies and the ferrets;
I cannot stand the frogs,
The budgies and the parrots!

The doctor thought a while,
And being quite a comic,
He broke into a smile
And slapped his bulging stomach:

'The things you cannot *stand*
Confirm my diagnosis -
I think that I have found
A case of 'p*sitt*acosis'.

Marguerite Pratt

The Eagle

The eagle looks for his prey
With his beady eyes
He plunges to the ground
He knows his dance well.

Cassie Knights (9)

SIMPLY BETTER

Life would be simply better, if all you people would
Let me decide what's best for you, and for the common good.

Life would be simply better, if you all would just decide
To let me make your decisions and forget your foolish pride.

Life would be simply better if nobody got ill.
I'd arrange for clever doctors to produce a perfect pill.

Life would be so simple if the starving all could eat.
Wouldn't people eating people ensure sufficient meat?

Wouldn't life be simple, if you gave me all the power?
I could watch you being obedient, from atop my ivory tower.

Wouldn't life be simple if only I could breed?
(I'd try to share it out a bit, and not run out of seed.)

Wouldn't life be better, if your cars weren't on the scene?
When riding on your bicycles, please avoid my limousine.

If I become your ruler, a ban on tractors will be made.
There will soon be full employment; for all those with a spade.

I'll holiday every other week; it's such hard work, decreeing.
When I've had enough of golf, I'll brush up on my skiing.

You'll simply never strain your brain; just obey me to the letter,
And every day in every way everything will be much better.

If I become your ruler, (And you know that it makes sense.)
I'll do exactly as I like, and balls to the expense.

Ed Mallinson

THE EMPTY HOUSE

The timbers creak,
And groan
Like an old man with life-time's tribulation
Meeting finally that camel's straw
Which added to his lot will send him to oblivion,
Or worse.

The air moves restlessly,
Although a breezeless day has reigned till now,
As though it's troubled in the mind
With anxious problems of a kind it can't reject.
Nor sleep to solve.

The gloom of darkness contrasts with the sun-drenched joy without,
Translates each murky corner into secret underworlds
Where entry is forbidden
On pain of loss of reason or of access into Hell.

Fear stalks the margins of your consciousness;
Demands firm resolution
And the shield of common-sense
To keep it nicely parted form its prey.

You don't believe in ghosts of course.

Yet now through all the intervening years
You vividly recall your proto-self:
A tiny child, curled up in bed, lying in awe
Of shadows on the wall
And shapes with meanings
Way beyond those visioned by their architects.
Is this so very different?
Is it really that the thicker shroud of adulthood
Does more than add the flimsiest of curtain-nets
To your respectability?

You don't believe in ghosts of course.

Once long ago they used to say that walls have ears.
These walls, and floors and ceilings too,
Have ears and eyes,
And no doubt touch and taste as well -
All seven senses that we ever recognise.
They use them now to monitor intruders,
And guard the long-departed occupants
Who mixed their souls
With prior-established plaster, bricks and mortar
And stamped their personalities through times
Upon the ambient space.

'Begone' they whisper silently.
Resentful, petulant.
Their power perhaps no greater
Than to create unease, pretend to menace,
And to strive from out their fabric
To resurrect those former denizens;
To manifest by psychic force their form;
And so confront you with their apparition.

You don't believe in ghosts of course.
Ignore such presence. They're not really there!
Only reflected shadows, residual noise
Left on a faulty tape you've just wiped clean.
The place is harmless:
Like a forest night
Or journey through a disused churchyard,
Where breathed suggestion boasts its glory hour;
Deploys its empire; puts reality to shame.

No call to think about it.
A strong imagination needs reasonable constraint.
It's normally not difficult
To exercise a rational view of everything you do.
Your right of entry was inviolate.
But still . . .

You've spent more time than you intended.
The world outside is beckoning.
You have no further purpose here
And other calls on your attention,
To which you'll gladly turn - no, not with pleasure
Or relief,
But with the warming satisfaction of duty put in train.

So with that promise of a lighter step
You make to leave
The empty house.

E J Nickson

Free To All

The sun is shining outside above
The birds fly all around us all day with
God's love,
The children play their silly games too
And the gardeners do what they also have to do,
They will cut the grass and dig their borders
And sometimes ask in guests and lodgers.
They have flashy cars and big houses too
but when you are in a tower block flat you
don't have these things to look after and do.
So take pride in your palace above,
even though it's small,
but just remember you are not greedy after
all like some at all,
You ask for so little but give out so much
but always remember that one day in
God's Kingdom above
You will be rewarded with much 'God's love'.

Carol Rutland

A Day Without Mirth (Is A Day Lost)

How dark the day, without laughter.
when one's mood, hits an all-time low.
But gloomy clouds, will change to blue,
when mirth, starts to overflow.
A merry heart - the medicinal balm,
is a tonic to start the day;
So mirth, must be the priority,
in our walk, along the way.
Should you see some people laughing,
just enquire, about the joke.
For when you've seen the funny side,
you will laugh, and be glad, you spoke.
When inspiration eludes you,
just doodle away with your pen.
And who knows, your composition,
could trigger laughter again.
Some whimsical words, will generate
the embers of a smile;
And you'll have done your bit, for
humanity, which will make your day
worthwhile.
So hold aloft, the banner of mirth,
with a slogan, bold and gay;
For laughter is the best medicine:
take a measure, every day.
A day without mirth, is a day lost:
Melancholy - a waste of time!
So I hope, I've got my message across,
in the best way I know - with a rhyme.

Patricia-Mary Gross

ECHOES AT ABERFAN (1966-1996)

Our village, pretty in normal times,
Chapels galore and shops-next-door.
The usual coal-tips stand around
Terraced houses and shuttered ground.

The big-tip stood above the mill,
Predominant like a brooding hill.
Beneath and past it ran our gurgling stream
Weakening its structure like a ghastly dream.

Again it rained and rained - like hell,
Incessant for days its doom to spell.
When will it stop? Why did it start?
What is its purpose but to break our hearts?

Man's greed, dug from beneath our hill
The 'slurry' that brought our lives such ill.
We'll never be able to turn-back that clock
Nor tighten the heart-strings now rendered slack.

The coal-tip's base slid silently at first,
Then 'whoosh!', engulfing everything in its thirst.
It swallowed us all, with saddened groans,
That ominous structure stole our once-placid homes.

We lost not only our treasured past,
But our future too, at our seed-corn's cost.
Those kiddies and their teachers stood
For everything about us that was good.

The next generation left us all that day,
Our debts in Heaven and our ills to pay.
A gap emerged, a void bequeathed,
The sorrow we shared, with tributes-wreathed.

Our little kiddies had trooped through their drill.
All our dreams at school to fulfil.
Bright eyes, happy laughs, their future to earn
From skills and knowledge we had yet to learn.

No more to hear their singing sweet,
Their pleasant laughter from every street.
Those 'tambourines' stay silent, the bells are stilled,
Skipping ropes lay limp and 'gazootes' untrilled.

Why should a tragedy like this occur?
What purpose is served when life becomes a blur
Of tears and anguish without end,
Seeing nothing but sorrow around each bend?

Can lives so shattered ever be unimpaired?
Will wives and mothers have their love repaired?
Will man's lack of foresight ever dispel
And avoid recreating this kind of Hell?

Friends abroad, to whom our village-name meant nought,
Reacted with horror at such sorrow wrought!
How could we leave a school to risk such woe
For five minutes, let alone for evermore?

Brian Harris

'Goodbye,' We Said . . .

'Goodbye,' we said. 'We've loved too much.'
Though we'd forget the gentle touch
  Of lovers' fingertips now parted
It is too late
To change our fate
  Or wonder why this love was started
When we were old we'd count the cost
In sleep we'd dream of the love we lost
And the ghosts of the memories that had to die
Would haunt those dreams when our tears ran dry.

Albert

OH MY ENGLAND

Oh my England
You will soon be gone
Oh my England
Hear my song

We are so sincere
Hear us loud and clear
For the greed of the few
Everything will be lost
All we hold most dear
Oh all at such a cost

Oh my England
You will soon be gone
Oh my England
Hear my song

What of the heroes
What of the past
Oh my England
Are we to become outcast
Let us prey for dear old England
Perhaps someone will hear us at last.

C Burrows

GONE AND DONE IT!

Well, what do you know?
She's really gone and done it then!
Surely not. Is that so?
She's really gone and done it then.
Do you think he'll follow her?
She must be round the bend.
Well, what do you know.
She's really gone and done it.

Doreen King

CIGARETTE

On a rainy day,
I saw her burn
Smoke spilled
lazily from a chimney . . .
(I felt guilty about my cigarette)
Then she drifts away from me again
Sat alone in the shut up room
but smoky eyes can't see the gloom
I've smoked myself sick,
Smoke stains my hands, evidently more
than she did alive, apparently
Day upon day, a hundred a day . . .
Shut up in a forgotten room
Sepia on her picture, my skin,
The flint wheel turns again
I wait to feel the cancer spread.
I wait to feel the feeling dead.

Kenneth Baird

OUR DIRTY WORLD

Countrysides full of corn and wheat,
Do not destroy them they're such a treat,
Keep our rivers clean and fresh,
Clear the canals of wire mesh.
Admire the lovely nature reserves,
They're places that we don't deserve.
Why do people drop all this litter,
With just one thought it could be prettier.
Think next time you drop a wrapper,
Who will pick it up after,
So instead of being so rash,
Pick it up and put it with the trash.

Jennifer Beeston (12)

The Village Of High Dudgeon

'Twas an ink black night in the village
And the rain came slashing down
There were thoughts of pillage and murder
In the head of old John Brown

He had sunk a few pints in the Chequers
Followed by a whisky or two
There'd been talk of bowmen and fletchers
And who was better than who

As the air got hotter and hotter
The bets were placed on the form
The challenges got wilder and wilder
On a Friday night just true to form

Said the fletcher I'll make you a bow man
Much better than arrows you make
What's more it will shoot further
Now let's see the size of your stake

This was more than Bill Brown could stand
For his bows were well renowned
If it's you that's making a challenge
It's here I'll be standing my ground

At that there were roars of approval
From the drunks and doxies all there
This looks like a fight to finish
To be settled right then and there

A yew stave was pinched from the churchyard
The fletcher set to work on the bow
By the fire was a bundle of hazel
They are good for arrows you know

Bill Brown selected a sapling
And with his knife he set to work
He whittled away for an hour
As patient as the old parish clerk

A cock from the back of the butchers
His feathers did he reluctantly lend
The carpenter ran for his gluepot
The feather and hazel to blend

The blacksmith made an arrowhead
With curses and flames all around
'Twas soon fitted onto the hazel
To cheers and drinks all round

Back in the snug the fletcher
Had been busy on the yew stave
A shaping and coaxing a bow shaft
His honour and money to save

By now they were all very merry
The beer had been swilling so fast
The landlord had entered the spirit
And poured water into the casks

It was half past twelve in the morning
The evening had promised so fine
Had changed to be really quite nasty
In fact it had turned into rain

As out of the pub they all staggered
The parson was holding the bets
He said the butcher should 'Do the honours'
As he slid a few quid to the vet

Up stepped the butcher all flustered
And fitting arrow to bow
Pulled the string to his ear'ole
And killed the farmer's best cow

The farmer of course he was angry
Best cows are not cheap these days
Bill Brown got the blame from the family
And now said the farmer 'You pays'

I placed all my cash on the wager
The parson said I have been robbed
The vet the sly old bugger
Had gone but should have been mobbed

This tale is a sad one I tell you
The moral is hard to relate
The bowman had made a curved arrow
Instead of making it straight.

J E Hobbs

WIMBLEDON CANCELLED

Sound of ball on cat-gut is obliterated by teeming down-pour,
the latter noise has become a deafening roar.

Usually people smile in the sun in June and July,
this year, the sun has passed us by.

People's faces as in winter months, wear a frown,
Oh, how cold and rain do get us down.

Anticipating the annual tennis fortnight,
through bad days keeps our hearts light.

Wimbledon brings a wave of fresh air,
A change from kicking a ball in stale air.

Rackets swinging only between showers of rain,
Will Tim ever get the chance to win and reign?

Luscious strawberries and cream swamped by water,
drowning gastronomic dreams of every son and daughter.

We'll remember this year's top tennis,
and we'll be reminded of Venice.

For every player, spectator, and tout,
Wimbledon 1997 was, a wash-out.

Joy R Gunstone

Leaving Childhood Behind

Lost in a world
of buttercups and daisies
where daytime is playtime
and life's just a joke.
Lost in a world
in a world that is lost
where strange sounds and illusions
make deception a game.
Lost in a world
where time conquers love
when the clocks strike the death hour
all feelings will perish.
When I was a child
I played in a meadow
the world outside was all blotted out.
Then I ran from the meadow
and found a wilderness
where the buttercups
wither at my touch.

Rhiannon M E Brace

Castle Green

When you are tucked up snug in Castle Green,
with patchy quilt and teddy bears
surrounded by 'housey' things,
colours, textures, patterns bright
and your light-emitting smile
I'll bring champagne and chips
and warm my heart before your lovely eyes
and love you as the light goes from the evening skies -
- when you are tucked up snug in Castle Green.

Alex Burns

Drink City

I don't want to miss the beat
I don't want to drop the pace
My throat is crying overload
Even though we're standing face to face

Drink City
No pity
The street dictates the rules

The nightlife pulses through me
The crowd shouts atmosphere
Excitement is what I need
Between all the poses and the beer

Drink City
No pity
The street dominates the fools

The bow ties control the lines
Sidewalks get a little mean
Pressure explodes so fast
As pain breaks out on the street

Drink City
No pity
The street's just out of school

Bad blood can not be tamed
Good times start right here
All troubles are washed away
By the promise of another beer

We all create the danger
As the night gets a little stranger

My brain is blinded by the lights
My body goes on for broke
The night is played to the limit
But the night is just a killing joke

Drink city
No pity . . .

Bernard Harry Reay

The Man Who Had Ten Toes

I knew a man who had ten toes -
he laid them on the line:
for all he cared there might have been
no more or less than nine.

He turned them in, he turned them out,
he never turned them up:
you'd find it hard to nail him down -
to him I raise my cup.

He tipped along from top to top
where tulip blooms are grown,
and yet I've never seen him forced
to tread upon his own.

He'd trip the light fantastic
till he was warm as toast:
yet he had never touched them once -
it was no idle boast.

He placed his cap upon his head
as soon as I had passed,
and then he turned upon his heel
and took to them at last.

Peter Watson

Shine On

It's dedication day with the Ajax team,
That bring about Sunderland's new dream,
It's time to name Sunderland's new park,
It's named by Murray who's such a bright spark,

Stadium of light he says it's to be
Not a name that would be thought up by you or me
So we will see if it lives up to its name
Or will it be so much of the same

So come on lads let the light shine
May the first division be entirely thine,
Throughout the season play with all your might
And go up as champions in the stadium of light.

D Reynoldson

An April Shower

As a ray of sun comes peeping through,
The bleak becomes a rosy hue.
Flowers lift up their wilting heads,
Spiders creep out to weave their threads.
Sparrows, finches, the snowy white dove.
All whistle and sing to the sun high above.
Rabbits, stoats, and otters too,
Come out and bask in the rosy hue.
Trees stand tall, leaves uncurl.
Then a raindrop falls, like a tiny pearl.
All goes still, flowers wilt in defeat,
Rabbits and stoats make a hasty retreat.
Birds fly into the trees again.
Taking shelter from this downpour of rain.

J Dragedore

Failure

The garden looks a sorry mess
After all the time I spent
Nothing's grown just as it should,
I won't have saved a cent.

I've sowed and tilled, just like it said
Worked hard, by any means.
But as I'm looking round the place,
I see blackfly has got the beans.

The greens! Now will they be alright?
I really have my doubts.
Clubroot has claimed the cabbages
Caterpillars on the sprouts.

The root crop may be better,
But, as I'm passing by.
I note that wireworm's got the spuds,
Carrots have carrot fly.

My hair is in confusion,
My clothes in disarray,
And all I have to show for it,
Are weeds, more every day.

It's all so disappointing,
Not worth my time, I know.
But, as the Good Book tells us,
We reap just what we sow.

S M Woodrow

Clinging On

I'm a town rook, I am
Only got one tree,
I live on beefburgers
Built my nest out of clingwrap and lolly sticks
Well, what would you do
If you wanted to survive?

I've taught the kids
To grab their food among the traffic
'Humanity' I've told them
'Is only a phase
We've loaned them the earth
After them, it's us'
Well, what would *you* say
If you wanted to survive?

Merle Tshiamalenge

8/1/97

Staring at walls
Staring at silence
and listening to music.
Still life
at 12.27 am
Living colours
in a dull silence
floating brightness
in a plain lifeless.
A dead room
with a hissing tape
and ticking clock.
Full stop.

J Kidd

My Love In A Mist

Of all the names that I like best
'Darling' is the one above the rest
I was called that by her I loved most
But now even the memory is just a ghost

For long ago she was taken from me
And it's only in photographs that I see
Her lovely face, extremely dear
From quite afar and yet, so near

Because my time is approaching its end
We'll be together, when for me God will send
Not as before that death can sever
But in a wonderful life which lasts forever

Our love will continue from my time of sorrow
That day years ago, when God took you to borrow
Until He calls for me my love hear my plea
I'll not be too long, so please wait for me.

Hal Takata

British Summertime

Home from the hols
Waiting in the taxi queue
Four ten am in the freezing fog
Welcome folks to the UK
Six hours late but only
Four before we go to work
No you can't hire the taxi
He's not airport registered
Now I know what queue rage is!
Over here mate, put your flag down,
Private hire, now for God's sake
Take me hooooome!

J Horsham

At Christmas Time

Christmas time there's so much fun we laugh and shout with glee
Shops full of things for us to buy so much for us to see
Christmas carols sung out loud 'Glory be goodwill to all'
Thinking of others in different lands hoping they hear our call
Cards to write presents to get remembering those near and far
Family, friends, aunts, uncles, grandma and dear grandpa
Days are short cold and grey but we do not notice these
We bustle around with a never-ending list amongst lit up
Christmas trees
Children write of toys they would like it never seems to stop
They are busy remembering all the things they saw in every shop
It's nice to ring our close ones we've not spoken to for ages
We even take to letter writing which go on to many pages
So many friends to visit at this festive time of year
Laugh and chat eat warm mince pies fill ourselves with cheer
As we sit down to eat our Christmas lunch a prayer is said to
all of those we have met and known
And at Christmas time again next year we hope that this has
grown and grown . . .

Lesley Dawn Garbett

Happy About What?

Tears are rolling down my cheeks,
I'm so happy I just can't speak.
My face is going slightly red,
My feet feel like solid lead.
I'm so happy I just can't say,
But let me tell you . . .
It's made my day.

Joane Lonsdale

Between The Lines

'A hundred lines by tomorrow,' now a hundred lives and not in straight lines either
time was infinite like the sky over our heads that sometimes flicked daylight all night when the rain was metal
sleep was in the head resting horizontal . . .
life before wasn't real anymore, school, youth; you were someone else now.
waiting and waiting in-between the noise that dimmed the silence, it was then
we all stood down against the offensive of life
a kind of amnesty like the stale gunsmoke of the early morn
mist drifted through us, each and everyone
when time fell silent . . . it was Christmas day.

T L James

Busy People

People are just like ants.
Scurrying to and fro.
Never taking time off
To watch a sunset's glow.
To even stop and listen
To hear a songbird up in the treetops high
They just go on hurrying and rushing by
They never seem to notice
A rainbow after rain
They only seem to find cause to complain
Doesn't it make you wonder
About this world of ours
And where, oh where have they gone
Those lost magical hours.

M Whittaker

Pet Talk

If only they could speak to us, our four-legged friends so dear,
We praise, rebuke and challenge them - no answer do we hear
Save an occasional bark or mew whose meaning's far from clear.

We greet them in the morning, and we kiss goodbye at night,
We cuddle, stroke and fondle them, we ask if they're all right,
For when in pain they cannot speak to tell us of their plight.

We trust them with our secrets - they will never tell a soul,
Whatever they may see or hear, they'll never be a 'mole',
Indeed, some reach 'purr'fection as they play the listening role!

Although they cannot speak, they can communicate with skill,
We can't mistake their message when they need another fill,
Or when demanding silence whilst they wait to make a kill.

They use their God-given senses well, they listen, look and learn,
They touch and pat, they sniff and taste, what isn't good they spurn,
They recognise our voice and tread and hear our car's return.

Some use their gifts to good effect to keep us safe from harm,
We hear of pets in burning homes who've raised the fire alarm,
Whilst sheepdogs prove invaluable controlling sheep on farm.

Some train to help us in the home or guide us in the town,
All give companionship and joy, and cheer us when we're down,
Being especially caring when we wear an anxious frown.

If only they could speak to us, I'd really like to know
What Katie did before she came to share our bungalow,
And why, when gathered in my arms, she fights and struggles so.

Where did she live when she was young? How come to be a stray?
Was she deliberately dumped or did she run away?
If only she could tell me, it would really make my day!

Perhaps, upon reflection, it's the fact they cannot speak
That makes our pets so loveable; no snide remarks, no cheek,
No arguments, no lies - just friendly barks, miaows and squeaks!

M A Sanders

A MAN'S BEST FRIEND

He looked at his dog fighting for life,
Was he to lose her, as he did his wife,
He patted his dog, then stroked its head,
As down his cheeks run tears he shed.

He stroked the dog and patted its head once again,
Whispered in its ear, this man has come to ease your pain,
A Vet then knelt down by the sick dog's side,
concern on his face, he tried best to hide.

The Vet run his hand along the dog's neck and then its spine,
The cause of the dog's pain, he found it hard to define,
He rose from the dog's side, seemed much deep in thought,
Then went over to a case that he had brought.

With a syringe from the case he knelt down again,
Inserted an injection to ease the dog's pain,
After patting the dog's head, the Vet got to his feet,
Saying he injection the dog had would help it to sleep.

Once more alone the man lay at the dog's side
Showing love and affection he could never hide,
Hands round the dog's neck, he looked up to pray,
Dear God, please let my dog live, let me have her, at least for
a few more days.

Leonard J Negus

WRESTLING IN THE NIGHT

You hit the pillow fit to yell,
For sleep will elude you 'till the early hours,
Your mind is racing - an active cell,
You have to admire its omnipresent powers.

A wish to relax, but all in vain,
A hopeless situation encountered before,
The constant drumming of the falling rain,
Sounds of a rock concert, the wind's steady roar.

The day's events go shuffling past
Like a one-armed bandit - a glimpse and gone,
Every thought in order but moving fast,
When sleep arrives remembering none.

And yet, you never recall that point in time
When the memory fades and the coma ensues,
Try as you must, the missing line,
You search the compartments for tell-tale clues.

Awake in the morning not feeling refreshed,
Struggling to make the body perform,
If only it could be full of zest,
Hiding the truth, clothes to adorn.

J M Fryer

OUR ARTHUR LEARNS STATESMANSHIP

Our Arthur?
Yes, Mum?
What d'ya chop cat's 'ed off for?
I didn't mum, didn't mum, didn't
Then what's it doin' 'ere in two bits?

I chopped its body off.

John Carley

Confusion

There's a stranger sat there in that bed
But it's got my dear mum's shell
Alzheimer's is what it's called
And it's got mum under its spell

I wonder what she is thinking
As she lies there in her bed
She looks all around her and mumbles
Just what's going on in her head?

She seems to still have thoughts
Though none of them for today
Her brain is still ticking over
Yet it's taken my dear mum away

It's all so very confusing
To see her sat there in her bed
For the mum I love has gone
And I'm grieving for her, like she's dead

Shirley Lidbetter

Emma

If her heart were on the outside
An English rose is what you'd see
Her face the like of a petal
Fallen from a cherry blossom tree
Her hair the image of stardrops
And sunshine on hazy days
Her eyes the glow of sapphire
Held up for God's array
But most of all her beauty
The likes I've never known
The Lord created my daughter
She is Emma, she is born.

Amanda Gordon

Poetry

Poetry you know me well,
What have you in store for me today,
My pen breathing with every move,
How would I write without your desires poetry,
Spelling the words my heart beats out,

Some are rainbows colours many,
Just as much are they sad,
Many just sweet memories,
Others clinging to crazy dreams,
Oh poetry so like a deep well.

Such wonders come from you,
Oh poetry who named you so,
Many a poem has been written,
Allowing one escaping time,
Seeing rainbows through the mind,

A refuge engulfing in you poetry,
Wiping away tears of sorrow,
Writing in you for hope in tomorrow,
Stay poetry with me, my pen's in hand,
Waiting for what you have to say.

Rosina Drury

Robert And Tracey

My robot's name is Robert
He came from far away.
He came down with an orange
But then Robert threw it away.
Robert had a banana friend
Her name was Tracey
But silly little Robert used to
Call her Stacey.

Charlotte Moulder

THE EVOLUTIONIST'S CREED (AND I DON'T BELIEVE A WORD OF IT)

From a hundred odd building bricks* chance built a Universe
Combining, re-combining chance completed the task.
With random profusion chance scattered out the stars.
Chance did all things. Why? You mustn't ask.

Chance then went on to fashion our world.
Fortuitous gases condensed and then swirled,
Chance can't say why or give any answers
Except that it took many millions of years.

With ceaseless perfection chance went on to make
Glory and beauty just for its own sake.
It was responsible for every separate thing.
The mystery of trees and the butterfly's wing.

Achieving the impossible, *chance* then gave us thought
(How it gave us what it didn't have is diligently sought)
No doubt they will teach you these facts when you're in college,
Chance made all the instincts too, for *chance* implanted knowledge.

Pure chance had mindless genius. Each thing that it did make
Was a wondrous perfection without a mistake.
So clever was chance, that scientific fanatics
Are still working out its laws-expressed in mathematics.

Is it not natural that men of great learning
Feeling perhaps empty, with an odd sense of yearning
Should worship this thing that hasn't got a mind
For it witlessly created the whole of mankind?

Dorothy Watkins

* Elemental atoms

Wee Flies In Their Eyes (Walking Down South In July)

I tramped down to the Lough where the fish jump high
Through a different world with wee flies in their eyes.
I rolled back in a hollow by a big fallen tree,
Closed my eyes to the sun and forgot about me.

I forgot about you in your media world,
All you whitewashed tombs and political herds
Who mill about lordly to sell us the facts
While peddling opinions you learned from the pack . . .

Past my best, in the quiet, every thought bled away
To the murmuring wash in the heat of the day.
Remembering nothing, I could see nothing more,
For my future and past fell down dead on the shore.

They dropped off me like mud from my boots in the sun,
For time has no meaning when the wandering's done.
I screwed down my old cap and laughed into the sky,
Risen free like the fish with wee flies in their eyes.

Samuel G Watson

Pulp

With pad and pencil poised upon my knee
A pensive thought sometimes occurs to me
This pencil and this paper once were tree . . .

When death came slashing at the pine
Who swung the axe to make this paper mine?
Norwegian, Finn or burly Scot
Felled that noble giant . . . and for what?
Does any word put down by you or me
Warrant the death of that so noble tree?

D Merrifield

A Special Dream

I had a special dream last night, I didn't want to wake
I dreamt we were together in a cottage by a lake
The trees were all in blossom, there were roses by the gate
Everything was wonderful, at last we'd met our fate.

In woods we walked so green and lush, we didn't have a care
The birds were singing merrily, a song for us to share
Rabbits scampered all around, each one with its mate
Everything was wonderful, at last we'd met our fate

The sun was beaming in the sky, not a single cloud in sight
We sat beside the lake for hours, till it was almost night
We laughed and talked and we held hands, then it was getting late
Everything was wonderful, at last we'd met our fate.

We wandered back to our little home, content with what we had
So full of love and longing we'd never again be sad.
We laughed and kissed as night drew on, a million miles from hate
Everything was wonderful, at last we'd met our fate.

It was almost dawn when your eyes met mine and we climbed the
winding stair
I longed to give you all I had, all my love with you to share
It seemed to explode, the love deep inside we knew we couldn't wait
Everything was wonderful, at last we'd met our fate.

A Craig

Faces

Faces tell stories, mouth, nose and eyes
Watch faces closely do they tell lies?
Or the whole truth? Or a little of each?
Watch faces closely you they can teach.

R S Dooley

TEABAG

I'm a tea bag in the teapot
Alone inside I sit
But when the water falls on me
I will have to do my bit

My mission is a short one
I must try and concentrate
As I only have one chance
For my perfs to percolate

At least I tried my best
And I'm sure you will agree
That now my job is over
You've a lovely cup o' tea

Please rinse me out with care
Don't rip my little jacket
And let me say a fond farewell
To my friends left in the packet!

Sharron Lyn Goodison

OUR RON

They've sent him upstairs
Or perhaps quietly lowered down
.He's received elevation
Or perhaps just lost his crown
They've made him emeritus
Or perhaps put out to grass
A man to look up to
Or perhaps one to by-pass
They've made him a saint
And he thinks he's a toff
But will nobody tell him
That they've pensioned him off.

Tony Sheldon

SUKY

My little cat she's snow white,
Although a kitten and still likes to bite.
She plays all day with a little ball,
Chasing it up and down the hall.
In the garden she likes to play.
But only in the summer months like May.
She had to go to the vets for a jag,
Her little tail, it did not wag.
Now she's home and getting better,
And of course the weather is getting wetter,
So in the house she must stay,
Which means she can't go out to play.
My little cat is *simply* the best,
Or at least, the best, in the whole of the west.

Jacqueline Currie (16)

THE UNKNOWN

Into the unknown
You have gone.
Into the infinite space,
My eyes search the darkness
Dimly I see your face,
And listening, hear you say my name.
Into the unknown,
Yet I am sure,
A veil, is all that is between,
Your gentle touch, still I feel,
Yourself, though no more seen,
Is everywhere, and so I walk serene.

Madeline Chase

In The Midst Of Life There Is Death

A little white coffin
Was brought from the church
In the hands of the top-hatted undertaker,
Behind it came the tearful mother
Her two young sons by her side
Looking onto their baby's coffin
Probably the newly born perceived with pride.
No formal hearse, but the tiny coffin
Was handed into the leading car.
Were they local I wondered
Or had they come from far?

Yesterday I had seen my niece's baby
A tiny 5lb baby girl
And in the same ward a new-born baby
Born that very morn
Two into the world
And one passing through:
Seems so transient to me and you
My parents lost their first child
At only three months old.
No life for such a baby
Before her blood ran cold,
No chance to play
No chance to see
The pleasures there were to be
It seems so sad
A baby's death:
Such a waste of new life to me.

Evelyn Burr

MOD FLASHBACKS

The swinging sixties I recall
Were fast and fun and loud,
With Mods and Rockers daggers drawn
In fashion gear worn proud.

As for myself, a Mod was I
Whose mini skirt grew shorter
As every day I hitched it up,
'Til daddy caught his daughter.

Look dear, he said, it's not like me
To start a row or fuss,
But for the sake of decency
Go downstairs on the bus!

At school we girls were summoned to
A lecture by the Head,
Who made us kneel and measured skirts
Too short - and you were dead!

Until we made a clever plan
To fool her we'd all lean
And bit by bit skirts touched the ground,
Though back view was obscene.

This worked for weeks, but when at last
Some gawky boy told tales,
We all got lines, but then got him,
I still can hear his wails!

The Beatles' songs were all the rage,
A new dance every week,
Excitement, youth, free love all made
The sixties so unique.

Irene Carter

The Fabric Of Life

In our misery we cry
Always are we asking why.
Why to us this had to come?
Why do we now feel so numb?
Then we stop and look up high
Right into the brightest sky
We fancy *You* are there with us
Your kindly face looks down thus
Your love with sorrow, takes our hand,
And we begin to understand.
That life is like a training ground
Where difficulties must be found.
There is a greater world than this
A world of love and truth and bliss.
A greater God we've never known
Who'll never leave us quite alone
And all our sorrows, loves and joys
He'll weave together with great poise
Into a fabric, he calls 'Life',
And we shall weather every strife
And looking back in later years
We'll feel the love and not the tears.

Betty Kettlewell

Not Alone

I sit in the dark although it is light
Feeling so afraid and alone
Remembering the colours, the shades, the light
Wondering where it has all gone

I hear a noise and it makes me aware
Something is moving towards where I am
I sit, all nervous wondering who's there
Feeling a nudge, I laugh, it's only my dog, Sam.

A Murdoch

A Poet For The Day

Today I think I'd like to be
a poet who writes naturally.
Who doesn't have to stop and stare
but plucks the words out of thin air.

So here I go, I'll now begin
What to write? Love, lust or sin?
Oh why won't words just come to me
like Wordsworth I would like to be

I have no daffodils to see
The clouds they wander without me
And looking out I find I still
Cannot compare with vale nor hill.

I think it's time for me to end
No deep and lasting words my friend
I know I'll always write for fun
Though never reach the heights of some.

Tomorrow is another day
I wonder what will come my way
No matter what my dreams may be
I'm sure I'll do it . . . naturally!

Wendy Forbes

THE WORLD TODAY

Sadness fills my heart when I see
the wiles of today,
Rape, murder, muggings where
people have to pay
For something not truly their bent,
Is there anything we watchers can
do where we're sent!

I loath to see cruelty being done to
a child
Who is so innocent not in anyway
wild
Enough to be beaten, take heed
Some day you heathen, you
may be in need!

The wicked treatment
of birds and beasts
These days sicken me when
Feasts are held and animals
forgotten
Those people I feel must be
completely rotten!

The fish of the sea are netted
so young
They have hardly had time
to twirl and bung
Around with their friends in the sea
Even nation's fight over time so wee!

Loathing of the people who are
not for life.
He cannot stand their wicked
strife
Many creatures of the earth they
willingly kill
To glibly laugh when life has
ebbed away, their skill!

Their time will come when
death do us part
A day of repentance might
come from the heart
My watching could turn
to lover and affection
Knowing they will go to God
and be part of resurrection!

Alma Montgomery Frank

MILFORD-ON-SEA

Where else would I be?
The island, the sea
The Needles, the sea
The gulls the sea
The yachts, the sea
The ferries, the sea
The trawlers, the sea . . .
Born on the prairies
Far from the sea
In Canada, my homeland
Where I should really be!
But I love the coastline
And Milford-On-Sea!

Ida Mary Thomson (Stride) Pressley

Malvern Hill

I climbed to the top of a hill today,
The top of a Malvern hill.
I scrambled and gambled, I pulled until
I could see the top was higher still.
But I climbed to the top of a hill today,
The top of a Malvern hill.

I climbed to the top of a hill today,
The top of a Malvern hill.
I passed the place of the burnt black grass
And I climbed and I climbed until at last
I got to the top of a hill today
The top of a Malvern hill.

God's at the top of a hill you know,
The top of a Malvern hill.
I cried to the Lord with the wind in my hair
I had the time and the space to stare
And I knew he was right, so I said it in prayer
As I stood at the top of a hill today,
The top of a Malvern hill.

Francis Charters

A Friendly Smile

It's nae fit ye dee
But the wye that it's deen
The good deeds in life,
Dinna need tae be seen.
If it's glory ye seek.
Well your nae in my street.
Try a smile for the outcast.
The next time you meet.

Sophia D Winchester

For Jock

Your cold, brown nose is on twenty-four hour alert
Standing by to welcome me or any other potential dog-walker to your home.
Your extrasensory powers primed to detect a doggie lover in a micro-second,
A positive signal triggering a frantic frenzy of furry energy to ricochet up the hall
Hitting the target with affectionate accuracy.

You prefer to travel in the front of the car
Smiling graciously at lesser canines who have to travel on paw
With one ear tilted attentively at the conversation in case you miss anything
Whilst jumping from front to back in an ear-washing relay.

And yet, even in the midst of your most dog-consuming rituals
A master of non-verbal communication,
You sense the sadness in my eyes
And give me the paw and cuddle of empathy,
Sympathetic slobbers christening me afresh with love.
As your rough tongue soothes my inner sores in the way your mother taught you to heal your own cuts.
You carry the boulders of hurt from my body
With the same determination as you carry me stones from the river at Portglenone.

We're a right pair you and I;
Cuddled together, not quite sure who's comforting who.

Fiona Dalglish

UNTITLED

His marbled glass-like eyes
Quickly snap shut
To the sound and smell
Of nearby
Danger.
The jagged dry texture
Of his camouflaged skin
Gasping in the hot sunlight
Too intense for his liking.

Beneath him,
The soft silky
Grains of the sand
Flowing gently between
His
Claw fingers,
It too slowly burning
Away at his delicate
But armoured skin.

A quick movement
Is needed
For him to escape
This infuriating
Discomfort.

The eyes open,
Bigger than his head.
Exposed to the strong
Rays of the sun.
The pupils constrict
But still he manages
To see everything
Around him.

A soft pink tongue
Escapes,
It captures
A tasty morsel;
This satisfies
His constant
Hunger and
Without hesitation
Stealthily scurries
To a safer spot,
And awaits the
Danger to pass.

Lorna McKay

THE PERSONAL TOUCH

When the time comes, and I have to die
I ask my beloved ones 'Try not to cry'
I've lived and I've loved you all very much
But I know how you'll miss 'the personal touch'
I'll always be near you wherever I dwell
Please remember our bodies are only a shell
It's the spirit that counts, for it never dies
Though I know that this world thinks we're not wise
To say there's a place beyond our blue skies
To believe is the thing, that's all we require
To a stronger belief, I always aspire
When this you have found, what peace it will bring
Throughout life's sadness a joy song you'll sing
'I give you my peace' said Jesus our Lord
Accept this and be glad, for He is the 'Word'.

A Gillmeister

On Moving Inland From Kent

Prancing waves
Dancing waves,
Entrancing, sending glancing blows
on sea wall,
Spray flying, soaking all before.
Oh! How I miss the sea.

Thunderous roar, deafening to our ears
Gigantic jets of sea foam rising high
in the air.
Oh would that I were home to
see you there.
To walk the beach in solitude
with surf so clean
And think of things that might
have been.

S D Sharp

My Cool Spider

I have a pet spider
And it lives in my hair
I take him to school
And he acts kind of cool.
He's good at English, Maths
And French
And when we go out he
Sits on the bench.
He's red and brown
Striped and hairy
And now he's asleep and lying
Down.

Sarah Ball (10)

A CHILD, A WOMAN AND A DOG CALLED HONEY

As a child she ran and skipped
Even giggled when she tripped

Now she lives in a darkened world
Can't even see a flower unfurled

As a child she *watched* both snow and rain
Loved to make tiny daisy chains

Now she just *hears* thunder and *feels* the sun
And yet admits a new life has actually begun

For golden agile *Honey* became her eyes
Warns her against shock and surprise

Oh talented friend with silken coat
                    and warm moist breath
You brought back *life* when she only wanted *death.*

Sylvia Lukeman

LIFE BEGINS

My reflection looks back at me
Is that a wrinkle I see?
Grey hairs are growing on my head
I think I will go back to bed
What have I done for my sins
Have I had too many gins?
I have been out late on a date
Maybe I should contemplate
I have been accused of being haughty
Maybe that's because today I am forty.

Kathleen Johnson

The Retired Escapologist

The food was good
He needed nowt
But still he felt
He must break out

There were no bars
That he could see
And anyway
He had a key

His wife, sweet gaoler
Did not know
How he missed
The old days so

And when the tunnel
He began
She dreamt not of
His secret plan

She thought it but
A garden pond
And not a subway
To beyond

He dug it deep
He dug it spacious
Through strata
Recent and Cretaceous

He dug until
He met one day
A tunnelling
The other way

A man who brushed
On by with glee
Who shouted out
I'm free, I'm free

He recognised him
With a sigh
It was himself
In days gone by

Neil Begg

MEMORIES

My childhood was a happy time
With comfort of a nursery rhyme,
And thrill of snow, of summer bright
My mum and dad with me each night,
The pull and tug of ventures new
And laughter often, tears so few,
Contentment in my world secure
To last I thought for evermore.
Then as these years gave way to youth
I searched excitement, love and truth,
The future held a magic power
Ambition burned each waking hour,
What folly wishing life away
Which should be nurtured every day;
But mid-life slowed this rapid pace
And footsteps slurred, no longer raced,
The water-wheel turned quietly
And family waves would lap round me.
Yet now that I am tired and old
I cannot feel the icy cold,
For memories like stars above
Shine and sparkle, bring me love,
I see those faces oh so dear
Forever here, forever near.

Elaine Beresford

LIZARD

The lizard stuck out a tongue
Sharp: glinting in fractions
signalling torture to hotel lounge.
Tourists puffing pink and sweaty
remarked at the depth of history,
broken like cheese into a sea
of centuries now parcelled
conveniently in golden sand;

And 'heat' hissed lizard
behind polished thick glass
reflecting damp ferns.
luscious cosmopolitan women turned
pages brown with worship.
Sister black crows
'Who knows' hissed lizard
to the cawing tunes of burnt adolescence.

A red flag flew,
ground still burned.
they came they went
lizard; was not concerned.

David Williams

SEDBERGH SUMMER

Velvet soft hills above Sedbergh
Their hidden clefts and folds
Echoing your flesh
That I remember so well.
Soft and sweet would rise the scent
Of wild thyme and clover
Their green flesh bruised beneath your body.

Helen Renton

TIME FOR A VOICE

Time for a voice
Sublime in your choice
Be seated
Be greeted with mellifluous noise

It breaks from silence
On a rhythmic grip
Moving quick
On a soothing trip

It dips,
It sips from a tune
A melody in bloom
It skips, it slips, it flips
Takes you to seventh moon

It gives words to expression
A touch, with intention
It's bold, full-souled, untold
Behold,
A tender life's impression

S B Zadeh

THE SUMMER SONG

The summer song
The lovely song
With its lovely tune
Makes you sing and sing
Till 6pm in the evening
With flowers growing
And small winds blowing
The summer song
The lovely song.

Zoe House (8)

WORDS PUT INTO RHYME

Words put into rhyme can sometimes mean so much.
If they come from inner feelings of beauty, love and such.
Especially if their purpose is to help another's plight.
Like the comfort of a guide dog, to one who has no sight.
We just take for granted the beauty that we see.
But to live in total darkness, how frustrating that must be.
Yet with a dog that's trained to help them overcome their loss of sight.
Blind people get from place to place.
As if *daytime* instead of night.

Larry Dean

SILENT WATERS

How still the night
How slow the flow
The waters glisten down below
Down below the waters flow

The moon appears and stars reflect
Sparkling waters take a rest
Salmon leap to gasp the air
The rod that kills, it is not there

Rocks stand fast as waters flow
Thrashing, thumping to and fro
Running wild against the tide
Rocks stand still, they do not hide.

Here I stand upon the hill
Silent waters drive the mill
Down below with silent drive
The moon reflecting from the skies.

Irene Crawford

My Garden

The pests that love my garden are ants
The snails and slugs
The greenfly and the blackfly
Earwigs and many bugs
They feast upon my lettuce
The cabbages and sprouts
Having a lovely picnic
When the birds are not about

So now I grow all flowers
But even then they call
Nibbling off the tiny shoots
They really have a ball
Little sparrows love the greenfly
They help me quite a lot
I do not use insecticide
In this my blessed plot

I sit and watch the butterflies
On buddleia tree and mallow
The bees search for the pollen
On catmint and the tallow
I see the swallows dip and dive
To catch the insects small
Acrobats in motion
The Lord God made them all.

Margaret Chadwick

SOME CHANCE OF CHANGE

Sitting in a saloon,
cradling flat ale,
ignoring idle chit-chat,
ordering a bottle of light
to liven a dull pint in a dull bar
in a bleak, back-street dive in London.
The pool table lamp sways as the
                              side door swings open,
a familiar face lit by the light of day
surveys the grimy den,
scouring for her prey. Spotted,
she saunters over, perching,
on the stool beside me.
'Some chance of change,' sniping,
telling me the odds,
'Might as well get me one,' relenting,
she swills cognac and low-cal coke like
                              a favourite tipple and
starts to rant and rave about
work and waste and horses for courses and
best friends, sisters, bosses, outbursts,
diets, dogma, a whole rigmarole
I never ever want to hear.
I have to go and
drip from darkness to light,
out away from lipstick stained brandy glasses and
plumes of smoke, like childhood chimney stacks and
a muttered threat of excommunication,
out and in to another dingy cave
where old folk rattle on
and try communication with someone who never wishes to hear
all their rambling tripe.
Some chance of change, and
I order a large, large short and shun the ever-advancing,
whispering crowd around me.

A F Lynch

CHILLI CON CARNAGE

Take a dwarf dog with a thin skull
A cat without hair
And a rabbit with ears longer than its body
Bring together with floured hands
And roll out on a flat surface
Take a collector of oriental ćompacts
An exuberant French woman with red lips
And a practitioner of forensic science
Season with salt and pepper
And stir into the master recipe
Take a large man with an unlit cigar in his mouth
An Italian stripper with the face of a nun
Add the violent husband of a teenage bride
Serve on heated plates
Or in wide soup dishes
Sprinkled with parsley.

M Bigland

IF I WERE . . .

If I were an eagle how high could I soar?
If I were a lion how loud could I roar?
If I were an elephant how long would I live?
If I were a fox how far could I run?
If I were a dolphin how deep could I swim?
If I were a blackbird how long could I sing?
And if I were a tiger could I bask in the sun?
But after all that, I'm still just my father's son.

Foy Kennedy

EXPECTING THE METER READER

When you leave your front door unlocked
Don't hide your money under the electric cooker grill.
Because if the thief or thieves don't find it,
The electric element will.

Wise words spoken
After the event
That caused me much trauma
And time to repent.

All's well that end well
The bank made full restitution
I have learnt a lesson though,
Also found a sound solution.

I read my own meter now,
And put the numbers on the door,
Lock up my house, go my way
Worry is no more.

Use of electric is costly
We hate to see the bill,
But when the electric cooker burns the cash
That was meant to render it nil
It's like biting off the hand that feeds it.
Nothing left, cessation, extinction.
Still.

Kathleen McSorley

Daisy

I am a little daisy
Growing in this bed
And all the flowers around me
Are way above my head

I know I shouldn't be here
Cause I'm not as nice as them
I'm just plain and bland and ordinary
All daisies are the same

The roses tower above me
With their petals big and red.
And their leaves are big as houses
Cause they keep me in the shade.

The night has gone and morning breaks
The sun shines in the sky
And all of nature does awake.
Another day is nigh.

Then people come to view . . .
The beauty of this bed
Kind words are not about me
But the other flowers instead.

I try to let them see me
As I sway from side to side
But no-one ever notices.
How much that I have tried.

Then a little hand appears
And lifts me way up high
A little girl has seen me
A tear forms in my eye.

Edward Moore

Part Two
Of The Mill

Shadows extend the tirade of tones
Before the mill, with coloured stones
Raised uneven by roots of trees
The changing way that time agrees
Some day the sails will fly
Of ghostly memories and time gone by
Whoever knew its fate with sorrow
So strong in life, it fades tomorrow
Time and tide shall surely say
Goodbye my friend, on its final day
Some day historians will prefer
By way of pen in verse refer
To enigma beyond, in rolling hills
There to fade, discarded mills
One alone by a placid stream
Remains forever, within a dream.

Gordon Jackson

Where Are All The Butterflies?

When I was a child,
I used to catch butterflies in a jar,
Where have they gone now?
Have they gone far?

I used to let them go of course,
Such pretty creatures flying all around,
Reds and blues, rusts and whites,
Fluttering gently to the ground.

Jennifer Jensen

Wellington Bomber

A fighting bird
stands on jacks
in a museum.
Touching the metal,
I rub my fingers over the concave holes
of enemy gunfire,
That swooped out of a burnt-out sky.
Time has bitten away at the wingless carcass
now fragile and disembodied,
A machine gun cage
Exhibits on a table top,
glass firing sights remain intact,
A child,
as if in an amusement arcade.
reinacts the pretence
of a threatening pursuit,
firing reels of rapid gunfire
with a killing sound
The propeller blades
stand above my head
I imagined spinning in
a red battled sky,
When time upon time
it released all the ruin,
above all that war,
crystallising the earth below.

Arfon Williams

DEATH HUNT

She suddenly heard it,
A blood-curdling cry,
The hunting horn,
Her throat went dry.

They were after her
And she knew it,
She stopped to listen,
Then she blew it.

They jumped upon her,
Quick as a flash.
'Oh, hurry up!'
She made a dash.

She saw the fangs
Coming nearer.
Their hunger pangs,
Life, growing dearer.

The horn blew again.
'Oh, no,' she thought.
'Hurry, hurry.'
For she knew of the pain it brought.

She heard it again,
That curdling cry.
The horn blew,
'Get on or die!'

Then, one of the hounds
Lashed out at her,
The blood on her coat,
Her precious fur.

Blood poured out of
That pain killing wound,
Blood . . . pain!
That fox is now doomed.

Claire Lacey

So Easy?

It was a New Year
To be a new start
Get my act together
But where should I begin?

There was the decorating
Still not finished, paste awaiting
Cupboards need sorting
Drawers overflowing
Garden in limbo
Letters need writing.

Get out more, get involved
            - in what?
            And where? And who for?

It was to be so easy
Just make up my mind
Get up and get started
The intentions are fine.

But the energy's not there
The weather is dreadful
The flu lingers on
Please hurry up Spring.

Mary A Slater

ALICE

Another place a moment in time.
Such a beautiful face, partly mine.
I met you all those years ago and you
Loved me come what may.
You chased away all fears I felt and helped me on my way.
And I loved you always throughout my life.
For you stood by me through trouble and strife.
There wasn't a time when you didn't care.
When I needed you, you were always there.
So caring and loving in everything you do.
It's hard to imagine this life without you.
Now the years go by and time will tell
But you're still the lady I know so well,
And I thank you God for a blessing as no other.
When you gave me an angel for my mother.

Sally Carpenter

THE COLLECTABLE TEDDY

Old Grandfather Ted sits comfortably in his chair
Elevated slippered feet in the air
He sits with a knowing smile on his face
Unfortunately he cannot move from his space

Sitting on the fireplace shelf
Looking very pleased with himself
Is the elegant old gent
With a watchful eye on our every event

He is King of all he perceives
But there is nothing he can achieve
For he has but a ceramic head
Grandfather is a collectable, a model, King Ted

Patricia A Williams

THE SURGERY

Our doctor tells us not to smoke
drink or eat too much red meat
get lots of exercise. Keep to
the proper diet. No. No. No. Don't fry it
Don't do this, don't do that
Maybe it's caused because you're fat
Smoking is another sin. So is drinking gin
or anorexia which makes you too thin
Temperatures tend to rise, unexpectedly,
while it's diagnosed as just another virus
Booze is definitely out, especially!
if you're suffering from gout
Sex! Well! Practised safely it's ok
unless you don't feel that way
Be careful when romping in the hay, for
all your allergies might stay making you
reach for your spray.
Asthma, arthritis, angina take away
your youthful exuberance and
the nurse and dietician, alongside
your physician could do with being
super magicians, curing ills without pills
But they and their receptionists
suffer aching backs and fixed grins.
So just remember this
they're just human beings too.
Susceptible like me and you.

Calliach

Vincent Van Gogh's Self Portrait
The Voice From Inside

I am here can anyone hear me?
I just want to say hello.
I want to tell you my story.
Not what others think they know.

This is my self-portrait.
Although it looks drawn and fierce.
I want you to take another look.
My story does not yet appear.

My beard is the colour of sunflowers,
It inspired me in my work,
But it also brought back to me,
All of my past and present hurt.

My eyes I painted in comfort,
Yet they also represent fear.

My mouth a word not spoken,
Yet wanting someone near.

My brow is frowning in anger.
Yet also rising in love.

The blue painted swirls around me,
Remind me of skies above.

The distant look upon my face,
Is my heartfelt emotion.

Shadowed by insanity
I can also feel devotion.

You see this is not just a lonely face,
Upon a nameless wall.

Behind there is a meaning.
And it's time to tell you all.

Lisa Reeves

MIRACLE OF LIFE

I stand alone, the sky grows dimmer,
A dusty bulb the only glimmer,
I watch in wonder, filled with awe,
As shadows lengthen on the floor.
The bay mare groans, her battle won,
Turns loving gaze on newborn son.
The foal lies wet, bewildered eyes,
Unstable legs, yet tries to rise.
Led by instincts centuries old,
Small hooves grip, but just won't hold,
He tries again, does not know why;
He only knows it's do or die.
Mare encourages, wicker soft,
Foal stands proud, he stands aloft,
Born to live. Born to run.
I wonder what he will become.
Eventer, jumper, hack or hunter,
Racehorse backed by eager punter,
They live their lives how we elect,
And fills me with a new respect.
Eleven months he took to grow,
From microscopic embryo,
To form a life that's so unique,
With perfect body, all complete,
This gift of life, this newborn foal,
Is nothing short of a miracle.

Debbie Neal

Summer

I walked along in the sunshine,
The trees were tall and green,
The flowers in the gardens,
The loveliest I had seen.
There were ripe fruits in the orchards,
And not a cloud in the sky,
The corn was a golden yellow,
And cattle in fields nearby.
A gentle breeze was blowing,
Butterflies fluttered past,
Bees were gently humming,
For summer had come at last.
I passed the little grey stone church,
And the bells have ceased to ring
Jesu lover of my soul,
I could hear the people sing.
Now the ever-flowing river,
With its banks so steep and bold,
There were little fishes swimming,
And a bridge that was so old.

Pearl Burch

The New Arrival

Would you like to take a peep?
Don't make a sound, he's fast asleep.
It's feet up for me, and a book to read
When he awakes he'll demand a feed

A baby? Oh no and really no bother
A wee little puppy who has just left his mother.

D Bowden

A COLD WET NOSE

I have a very special friend
A friend I cannot see
And this very special caring friend
Was chosen just for me.

He's always close beside me
He's always by my side
And I know that I can trust him
To be my sighted guide.

As we walk along the pavements
Through wind and rain and snow
A cold wet nose and a furry head
Are all I need to know.

Jenny Nisbett

BONES AND STONES

(An ode to Jacob's Ladder, Cheddar Gorge, England.)

Pause thy manly mobile bones,
Take ease upon those aged stones,
Breathe calm between thy toiling groans,
And hush to hear harmonious tones -
'Twas life that walked they fossil bones,
And time that turned them into stones!

They paused betwixt their toiling groans,
Heard calm celestial angel tones,
Then gladly laid their aching bones,
Accounting for their lively loans -
Inscribed their names on ancient stones,
For life was e'er in bones and stone!

Edward Chalmers

To Harry

You are the first spring sunshine
That streams through the window
After a grey, cold winter.
You are the delicate violet
That blooms so suddenly and sweetly,
The first primrose, nodding in the wind.
You are the unexpected laughter
On a solemn day, the blackbird song
Carried on the breeze, softer than
Kitten fur, brighter than the stars
All the joy of life is in your smile,
No sorrow, yet, to show.
Innocence and trust are in your open arms.
The future is held in your open hand.
You are the undeserved benediction
In all of our lives.

H McQuirke

Loneliness

Life is such a lonely place,
When there is only one,
There's no-one there to talk with you,
When all your day's work's done.

But you can talk to God in prayer,
Whenever you feel blue,
And you will find He's always there,
The friend, that's always true.

So talk with Him when you feel down
Just don't sit down and moan,
For after having talked with Him,
You'll find you're not alone.

R Hart

A Fighting Tree

Leaves scattered small not big along each and every little twig
Irresistible sprays half displayed.
Numerous flowers bloom per sprig appearance almost too big
Dragged down each branch is made, into a brightly coloured shade,
Attenuated by young girls, some prig, who can't resist snatching
a sprig.
Changing her emotional sizn from abundance to decline.
Out in the scarce forest sun, of non-human life-form, one
Living mostyly a silent time in a seemingly endless wavy line
Equally amongst many, there's one, who feels superior to none.
Magnificent little beauty so divine, amongst the tallest of the pine.

Alone scattering petals for a bed, here only she has leaves to shed.
Nearby no other deciduous tree is seen, only the majestic evergreen
With branches high in heaven's air, no shade for them to dread up there.
Roots burrow deep unseen to where the dead men dream.
Isolated in life she battles ahead, for she desires her strain to spread.
Terrible devils who have torn her flowers, wear a human form.
Eventually she hopes in time her woodman will come to thin the pine.
Suddenly that day does dawn, sunlight ensures she is reborn
Intrepid she, when undermined, becomes amazing once unconfined.
This flowering tree her branches shorn, awakes to greet a new
spring morn.

Linda Dagmar Coleman

Worse Things Happen At Sea

My friend kept complaining of a sore knee -
I explained to him that worse things happen at sea.
I then related a story -
Of a man who was eaten by a shark
And after this his attitude changed -
And he began to be more realistic -
About his present state of health.

Stephen Dipré

Puss Puss

Pretty pussy pennant tail waving exciting through the cat-flap
to finalise his purring day
Pity the birds the sparrow the blackbird and thrush who
trustingly hop across his way
No conscience of cruelty manifests in this cherished bundle of
fur our family pet
Puss is missing late for dinner, puss puss we call as we
frantically hunt call and fret

We tell ourselves that stalking is natural for puss, then we
see the blood-torn feathers
Nasty horrid cruel cat we can see you skulking there despoiling
newly grown heathers
Belly grazing crouching waiting swearing ready to pounce on
some unwary luckless prey
All our protesting gone unheard, we reconcile ourselves with
the thought this is nature's way
Cunning cat purring its way into our affections rubbing
all seductive around our gait
We know we are going to forgive puss for his feline cruel
sadistic innate trait
Eager to welcome sweet pussy back into the warmth of the
loving family fold
A saucer of milk some choice cat-bits. Our reward a contented
pet to stroke and to hold.

G Graham

Circumferentially Challenged?

Why use other words
When infanticipating
Says it all for you?

H Wallace Gandy

I Follow A Dog's Behind

They look with wicked eyes,
At me who they adore.
Caring not for my weary sighs,
As with leads I make toward the door.
In leaps and bounds they race,
I follow at a snail's pace.
They love the wind if it blows and roars,
I follow and the rain it pours.
In snow they run and play with ease,
Me I follow and I freeze.
There they go running on ahead,
God I wish I was tucked up in bed.
One dog is not enough,
I have two and I'm out of puff.
For all the aches and pain
You will find me here tomorrow again
For I follow a dog's behind.

E C Inkpen

Memories

Oh! How we yearn for the days gone past,
how we laid, in the long tall grass,
gazing at the clear blue sky,
on a hot summer's day a gentle breeze,
whispering thro' the trees, sweet murmurings
of the bees as they flit among the leaves.
How peaceful it seems, just to lie and dream,
of all that might have been.

Eileen Scaplehorn

For My Baby Boy, Nathie Lawrence

That morn you informed me 'I'm on my way!'
Was . . . how shall I put it . . . an eventful day.
You see the surprise of you was a luminous moon.
This life to be born, expected next June.

Your Daddy amazed! Astounded! Quite dumb!
Lying together that night, wrapped tight, most numb.
For how you managed to turn the line blue
Could not be grasped, neither of us knew,

The abstruseness elapsed, the months thrust on.
The delightful wonder of a daughter or son.
The Siemens monochrome, a God-given sight.
The result so worthy of my poor bladder's plight!

Then that first miraculous sound via the hand-held Sonicaid.
Butterflies shared your home within as on the bed I laid.
The harmonious sound of ten beats to the dozen
Mine and Dad's head left simply a-buzzing!

Then three weeks before you came, the doctors weren't happy.
Mummy not well, clinging to Daddy.
My arms like pin cushions, feeling drained of my blood
You nearly ready to be born, to flourish like a bud.

Just like your sister, punctuality a demand!
Just *as* with your sister, I crushed Daddy's hand!
But I must now admit it, it wasn't that bad.
It was really quite 'joyous', no reason to be sad.

It didn't take long, not long at all!
The midwife so friendly; oh such a 'ball'!
Epidurals and pethidine I simply refused,
With Daddy beside me inner-strength was renewed!

At 02:49, my head was a daze,
At 02:50, my insides ablaze!
At 02:51, 'Just one final push'!
At 02:52, you arrived with a rush!

A boy! A boy! I first saw your back.
So blue, so slippery, with colour such a lack.
You proceeded to whimper, I knew you were fine.
Then at last you were cut from your nine month lifeline.

The pain simply elapsed as I held you close,
Such tiny hands, blue eyes, and a squidgy nose!
For this was the moment, I'd waited so long.
My heart within danced a beautiful song.

Your presence so wondrous to all who were near.
Just to look at you sleeping dispersed my eyes with tears.
Your sister so proud of her new baby brother,
Her love for you simply like no other.

But three months on, black thunderclouds threatened,
Your condition they told as my ears became deafened.
For all I wanted was to block the day out.
But no! It seemed things would be different from now.

Mummy and Daddy were frightened, so scared,
To plan for next year was something not dared.
'His heart's on the right; we'll have to do tests'
And for the next seven weeks we simply couldn't rest.

My sweet baby boy, inside I was crying.
But not on the outside, how hard I was trying.
You looked so tiny with wires attached to you.
It became like a gamble; would we 'win', or would we 'loose'?

But God shone down on His Sweet Little Child.
When we learnt you'd be fine, oh how we cried!
Your strength and your fight have been proven to us
But will even *you* learn to say 'Dextro-cardia with situs inversus'?

I think of your name, and how apt it seems.
As I look at your face radiating such beams.
For 'Gift of God' is the definition of Nathan
And you most certainly have travelled from Heaven!

So now maybe Son, you'll make sense of your nickname.
The one to which you'll allocate us blame!
We've already shared some nine months of fun
With our f*our-leaf clover*, our *one in a million!*

Always my love,
Mummy
xxx

Tracey A Jackson

TIME TO THINK

A quiet day,
A space in time
To think of things immediate
And then let thoughts go out
To family, friends and those in need
Beyond to the unknown future
To Him who holds the universe together.
One travels far on a quiet day.

Phyllis Moore

GLOOMY DAY

*G*loomy days are terrible,
*L*eaving the nice warm house,
*O*n Monday it's always gloomy,
*O*aks don't look pretty on gloomy days,
*M*ad traffic jams,
*Y*ou get stuck in.
*D*ebts to pay,
*A*nd bills as well
*Y*ou always hate gloomy days.

Lisa Sarah Newbatt (10)

THE GUIDE DOG

She waits, holding the lead.
Her guide dog sits waiting patiently
for the pull to get up.

Different body, but almost part of hers.
She walks safely across -
The oncoming traffic, rushing with full speed
slows down and stops.

Where would she be
but for her eyes, the guide dog,
perhaps sitting forlorn in a room
lost to the world.

Shanta Nair

MY GERBIL

Her fur is like gold
Her belly as white as snow
Her eyes are like rubies
And pink for her nose.

She hops like a kangaroo
She runs like a hare
I'm told she's a rodent
But I don't care.

Her tail is like a sausage
The way she eats is funny
Her teeth are like snippers
Yes, her name is Honey.

Victoria Wilkinson (12)

A Day At The Seaside

Candyfloss and seashells
Ice-cream and salty smells
Postcards lined up on racks
Kiss Me Quick fancy hats

Cockles, whelks, fish and chips
Round the bay tourist trips
Laughing policeman's noisy cheer
From the arcade on the pier

A coin to gaze miles out to sea
Shrimps and prawns ordered for tea
Paddling with shingle beneath the feet
Daring to jump each wave we meet

Donkey treks along the beach
Amidst the striped deck chair seats
Sticks of rock on all the stalls
And massive coloured plastic balls

Buckets and spades to make
Sandcastles for the tide to take
Jellyfish swimming into shore
Crabs appear with tiny claws

The big wheel turning round
The water chute plunging down
Check your weight the man was shouting
All this in a day's Sunday School outing.

Mo Brown

Secrets Of The Seashore

The battered rocky shores
And the gently flowing brackish creeks and lagoons
Hold all the secrets of the seashores.
Birds, mammals and fish, worms and shellfish too.
The cliffs are often rich with wild flowers
All is there for us to view.

Nobody notices all these marvellous things
They think it's a park without the slide and swings
They build sandcastles and swim in the sea
The seashore is a wonderful place
Please open your eyes and see.

Sharon Allison

Love Divine

Beyond the veil I see you clear
Smiling, oh so dear
Lovingly, as before
Yet divinely more

In my deepest despair
You are there
Soothing my sorrow
Promising tomorrow
Our love for e'er.

Pray soon you'll come
And put your hand in mine.
Allaying my fears
Ending my tears
With eternal love divine.

Alan M Duncan

Slate

Bowed shoulders hunched against the spiteful rain,
Sharp nose a-dip with each, still-steady stride;
Like the curved prow of a clipper carrying grain
To Liverpool; the old man trudges on, his pride,
His power, burning lower in his chest
But warming still, his heart beneath his vest.

'OK Dad!' (His daughter) 'doctor said,
That two miles every day would do you good
So wrap up warm - you're scarcely out of bed
And post this card to Olwen if you would,'
Knowing this ruse, this petty little crime
Would take him off her hands 'til dinner time.

He pauses by the cemetery gate
And whispers to her ghost beneath the sod,
'Not long Megan! Not long now to wait
Until I join you in the lap of God'
And hears the clear response 'Come very soon
We'll have a randy second honeymoon.'

He slats the water from his ancient cap
And winces at the thin, translucent claws
That once were hands. Hands that used to snap
A pick helve! Like a shaggy grizzly's paws
That once, to save a sticken, screaming mate
Had heaved aside a half-ton slab of slate.

He'd paid for that! A precious day's pay docked
For every day he lay upon his bed
While lovely Megan patiently unlocked
His spine with kaolin, like molten lead;
And wintergreen; ung methyl sal; the name
Though Latin, sounding Cymric all the same.

Lumbago dogged his footsteps after that,
Burning him while, from his flaxen rope
He ranged the quarry face like some huge bat,
Barring down. His daily, pious hope:
The Dust would never get him and praise God
It never did. His back gives him a prod

And on he goes. Down Stryd y Bont and past
Bro Dawel where his Megan used to live
Before they married; fetching up at last
Beside 'Yr Engan'. What he wouldn't give
To see it open once again and hear
'Myfanwy' through a haze of smoke and beer.

Some hope! He probes the brambles with his stick
To wake dead tenors, rotting in the shards
Of broken glass and sniffs the dank air, thick
With memories of dominoes and cards.
Then turns his back on golden days of yore
And strides his way, more shrunken than before.

Y Swyddfa Bost! he rams the postcard home,
Like a shot-firer tamping down a charge
And blasts Olwen from hell to kingdom come
And damns the bloody raining world at large
And stomps off homeward, feeling, in his ire
A little warmed by anger's healing fire.

Not much more torture now. The seeping rain
Which lately soaked the wattles of his chest
Runs off his coat-tails, adding to the pain
Behind his knees. The thought of warmth and rest
Spurs him off. He'll catch his bloody death
If this goes on. He pauses, short of breath.

Do him good? More likely do him in!
And good for what? Good for another walk?
Good for another dose of medicine?
(She doesn't know it's whisky mixed with chalk)
Ah! Soon he'll drowse the fire out. Success
Stuffed full of cottage pie and loneliness.

Tony Jennett

UNTITLED

As I sit in my garden
On a lovely summer's day
I see the beauty of our God
In the flowers that are so gay
I can see God's creation
In the butterflies and bees
And all the little birds singing high up on the trees
How wonderful to know our God
Who cares for you and me.

C J Connell

INFORMATION

We hope you have enjoyed reading this book - and that you will continue to enjoy it in the coming years.

If you like reading and writing poetry drop us a line, or give us a call, and we'll send you a free information pack.

Write to :-

Poetry Now Information
1-2 Wainman Road
Woodston
Peterborough
PE2 7BU
(01733) 230746